Eat & Explore
Minnesota

Eat & Explore
Minnesota

Christy Campbell

Great American Publishers

www.GreatAmericanPublishers.com

TOLL-FREE **1-888-854-5954**

Great American Publishers

P. O. Box 1305 • Kosciusko, MS 39090

TOLL-FREE **1-888-854-5954** • **www.GreatAmericanPublishers.com**

ISBN 978-1-934817-15-5

First Edition
10 9 8 7 6 5 4 3 2 1

by Christy Campbell

Front Cover Image: Mark P. Anderson, Big Whiskey Design Studio
Back cover image: Fishing near Brainerd, Minnesota
Back cover food image: Think Stock Photo ©Monkey Business
Chapter opening photos, istockphoto.com: Appetizers & Beverages p9 © Smokingdrum
Soups Salads & Breads p33 © funwithfood • Vegetables & Other Side Dishes p75
© Diana Didyk • Meat & Seafood p119 © Ezhicheg • Desserts & Other Sweets p181
© Edward ONeil Photography • Index p245 Think Stock Photo

Every effort has been made to ensure the accuracy of the information provided
in this book. However, dates, times and locations are subject to change. Please
call or visit websites for up-to-date information before traveling.

To purchase books in quantity for corporate use, incentives, or fundraising,
please call Great American Publishers at 1-888-854-5954.

Contents

Introduction 7

Appetizers & Beverages. 9

Soups, Salads & Breads 35

Vegetables & Other Side Dishes 91

Meat & Seafood. 125

Desserts & Other Sweets. 177

Index of Events & Destinations 246

Index of Recipes 255

Introduction

Just as I do with each state addition to the EAT & EXPLORE STATE COOKBOOK SERIES, I spent time learning the basics about Minnesota. As the book began to unfold, I discovered it to indeed be "The Star of the North." Being born and raised in the South, the northern part of our great land has always held a certain fascination for me. I would imagine America's early explorers traversing icy lakes, winding through forests of snow-covered pine trees and forging through uncharted valleys. The dangers of the extreme cold for these first settlers would have been great, so what made them stay? As I unfolded layer after layer of this magnificent state, the answer became evident. They stayed because of rich resources, amazing natural landmarks, and a call to their souls of the community they could build in a land of such beauty.

During the time spent discovering the treasures held in the "Land of 10,000 Lakes," I would imagine what life would be like living in an area so different than my home in the South. What I learned was delightful, because although the climate is indeed different, the similarities are immense. The warmth, openness and kindness of each person I had the honor of working with made me coin a new term in my mind — Northern Hospitality. I remember one conversation in particular I had with Ms. Sue Trinka of Detroit Lakes. We were discussing various events that occur during the Polar Fest celebration. Her love of the area and her desire to share it resonated with me during the remaining time I spent working on this book.

With each step of my journey through "The Star of the North," I began to paint a picture in my mind. The picture includes bowls of ripe red apples in family kitchens, dinner tables with hot soup to warm chilly hands, and the aroma of delicious food wafting through the air while strolling through county fairs. *Wild Rice Soup*, *Spicy Minnesota Spread*, *Bucky's Lefse* and *Cove Point's Lucca Pasta* are local favorites welcome at every meal. The deliciousness continues with *Christmas Stewed Fruit*, *Swedish Meatballs with Gravy*, *Easter Pizza* and *Orange Glazed Mini-Muffins*. However, people who know me well know that anytime I pick up a cookbook, I go right to the dessert chapter. I encourage readers of this book to do the same. *Chocolate Bread Pudding*, *Key's Café All American Apple Pie*, *Buckeye Brownies* and *Baklava* are terrific examples of why many say we should always have dessert first!

With this book, we enter into the sophomore stage of the EAT & EXPLORE STATE COOKBOOK SERIES. Although, like the early explorers, we are no longer traveling through uncharted waters, creating cookbooks is a learning process. It requires tremendous teamwork and I could not do half of it without the hardworking and always cheerful staff at Great American Publishers. We examine each and every aspect of how to make our company great, each person playing an integral role in our success. At the helm of each day is Brooke Craig, whose keen instinct guides the books in and out the door. Krista Griffin, author of the fabulous cookbook *Family Favorite Recipes* (check it out, it's terrific!) and Nicole Stewart keep their fingers on the pulse of retail sales throughout the country. Another author, Anita Musgrove, (*Alabama Back Road Restaurant Recipes*) looks into the nooks and crannies along America's scenic routes, discovering the places "where the locals go to eat." Diane Adams, with the help of Tori Kelly, makes sure the office runs as a well-oiled machine. Last, but certainly not least, are Rose Ellis and Christy Campbell (yes, there are two of us). Every day I am in awe of what these industrious women are able to accomplish. When people come to work, they do it carrying the weight of the challenges in their non-workplace lives. Rose has been a shining example of moving forward through life's hills and valleys. Christy Campbell, otherwise known as Christy Kent, has touched me with her radiant glow that puts a calming hand on the high-energy publishing world.

I want to give special recognition to several people who were vital to the creation of *Eat & Explore Minnesota*. Nikki Shoemaker gave it arms and legs, Cyndi Clark gave it presence, and Sheila and Roger Simmons gave it heart. I am forever grateful for these smart and talented people, without them this book would not have been complete.

With each year, as the EAT & EXPLORE STATE COOKBOOK SERIES grows, my family grows up right along with it. I can see my 9 year old son Preston, with his booming smile and big laugh, careening down the big waterslide at Edgewater resort. My mind's eye pictures my 10 year old son, Michael, studying each and every exhibit at the Science Museum. And as always, my beloved husband Michael is there, keeping a protective and watchful eye over our family.

The remarkable state of Minnesota is the fourth stop on our winding tour across this great land. Northern Hospitality is now firmly planted in my mind, and I know it will be firmly planted in readers' hearts. Thank you for traveling this journey with me as we continue on exploring… Minnesota.

Christy Campbell

Appetizers & Beverages

Hot Corn Dip

2 tablespoons unsalted butter, divided
3½ cups corn kernels (4 ears fresh)
½ teaspoon salt
⅛ teaspoon ground black pepper
1 cup finely chopped yellow onions
½ cup finely chopped red bell peppers
¼ cup chopped green onions
1 jalapeño, seeded and minced
2 teaspoons minced garlic
½ cup mayonnaise
4 ounces shredded Monterey Jack cheese, divided
4 ounces shredded sharp Cheddar cheese, divided
¼ teaspoon cayenne pepper

Melt 1 tablespoon butter in skillet over medium high heat. Add corn, salt and pepper. Cook 5 minutes, stirring constantly, until kernels turn deep golden brown. Transfer to bowl.

Melt remaining butter in skillet. Add yellow onions and peppers, stirring often until onions are wilted, about 2 minutes. Add green onions, jalapeño and garlic; cook and stir 2 minutes or until vegetables are softened. Add to corn mixture. Add mayonnaise, ½ Monterey Jack and Cheddar cheeses; mix well. Add cayenne pepper. Pour into baking dish and sprinkle with remaining cheeses. Bake 10 to 12 minutes at 350° or until bubbly. Serve with tortilla chips.

Albert Lea Convention and Visitors Bureau

Appeldoorn's Beer Cheese Dip

1 pound aged Cheddar cheese
1 pound mild cheese
2 cloves garlic
2 tablespoons Worcestershire sauce
Dash Tabasco
9 ounces beer
¼ teaspoon dry mustard
½ teaspoon monosodium glutamate

Grind cheese and garlic. Add remaining ingredients slowly. If beer is added too fast mixture may curdle. Let mixture stand in a cool place for 2 hours to blend flavors. Serve with chips.

Appeldoorn's Sunset Bay Resort

Chili Cheese Dip

1 pound lean ground beef
½ cup chopped onion
1 (16-ounce) jar picante sauce,
    mild
2 (15-ounce) cans refried beans
1 cup sour cream

½ teaspoon chili powder
Salt and pepper to taste
8 ounces Cheddar cheese,
    shredded
Jalapeños or mild chile, chopped,
    to taste

Brown ground beef with onion; drain. Combine all ingredients in slow cooker and cook on low 3 to 4 hours. Serve with vegetables or chips.

Bloomington Convention and Visitors Bureau

Texas Salsa

1 can pinto beans, drained and
    rinsed
1 can black-eyed peas, drained and
    rinsed
1 can corn, drained

1 cup chopped celery
1 cup diced green onions
1 small jar pimentos, chopped
1 small can black olives, chopped

Combine all ingredients in medium bowl. Mix well.

Dressing:

1 cup canola oil
½ cup cider vinegar

¼ teaspoon pepper
½ cup sugar

Combine oil, vinegar, pepper and sugar in saucepan. Bring to boil,
stirring till sugar dissolves. Pour over vegetable mixture. Refrigerate
overnight. Drain and serve with chips.

Chickadee Boutique

Fresh Guacamole

3 ripe avocados
½ small onion, finely chopped
1 garlic clove, minced
⅛ teaspoon chopped fresh jalapeño chile
1 tablespoon lime juice
⅛ teaspoon hot pepper sauce
Salt and pepper to taste

Mash avocados, coarsely, in medium bowl. Stir in onion, garlic, chiles, lime juice and hot pepper sauce. Season with salt and pepper. Chill, covered, until ready to serve.

Jeraldine Gustavson
Stand Still Parade

Taco Party Dip

1 pound Jimmy Dean sausage (regular or hot)
1 carton Velveeta cheese
2 cans Rotel tomatoes and green chilies

Brown sausage in skillet; drain and set aside. In a saucepan, combine cheese and Rotel. Cook on low until cheese is melted. Stir in sausage. Pour into large bowl and serve with tortilla chips.

Glenwood Chamber of Commerce

Bean Dip

2 cans white corn, drained
2 cans black beans, rinsed and drained well
1 cup ranch dressing
½ cup Italian dressing
1 teaspoon chili powder
1 small onion, chopped
1 teaspoon hot pepper sauce
½ teaspoon black pepper
2 teaspoons fresh cilantro, optional

Combine all ingredients. Serve with tortilla chips.

Hyde-A-Way Bay Resort

Mississippi River in Little Falls.

Zig's Hot Artichoke Dip

2 cups chopped artichoke hearts
1 (3-ounce) can chopped green chilies
½ cup salad dressing
½ cup shredded Parmesan cheese
? teaspoon cayenne pepper
Salt and pepper to taste

Combine all ingredients and mix well. Portion into 2 to 4 ramekins and bake in oven at 350° for 15 minutes. Serve with plain tortilla chips.

Executive Chef Terry Dox
Ruttger's Bay Lake Lodge

Artichoke Dip

1 (14-ounce) can artichoke hearts, drained and chopped
1 cup grated Parmesan cheese
1 cup shredded mozzarella cheese
¾ cup mayonnaise
2 tablespoons chopped green onions or parsley

Bake in lightly sprayed 1½-quart casserole, uncovered, at 350° for 30 minutes. Serve warm with crackers.

Char Johnson
Stand Still Parade

Feta Cheese and Pistachio Spread

2 large cloves garlic, minced
½ teaspoon salt
12 ounces feta cheese, crumbled
1 stick butter
¼ cup chopped pistachios
¼ cup thinly sliced chives

Mash garlic and salt into paste and combine with feta cheese, butter, pistachios and chives. Chill 4 hours. Remove from refrigerator early enough to serve at room temperature. Serve with sliced French bread or crackers.

Robin Berchulc, guest
Bear Paw Resort

Toasted Almond Party Spread

1 (8-ounce) package cream cheese, softened
1½ cups shredded Swiss Cheese
⅓ cup Miracle Whip
2 tablespoons chopped green onion
⅛ teaspoon ground nutmeg
⅛ teaspoon black pepper
⅓ cup sliced almonds, toasted

Preheat oven to 350°. Combine all ingredients. Mix well. Spread mixture into a 9-inch pie plate. Bake 15 minutes, stirring after 8 minutes. Garnish with additional almonds, if desired. Serve with assorted crackers or pita chips.

Chickadee Boutique

Spicy Minnesota Spread

2 (8-ounce) packages cream
  cheese, softened
¾ cup sour cream
½ cup hot salsa
1 cup fresh chives

10 drops Louisiana Hot Sauce
Dash of salt
1 cup finely shredded
  Cheddar cheese

Mix cream cheese and sour cream together until blended.
Add salsa, chives, Louisiana Hot Sauce and salt. Spread on
plate or tray. Cover with Cheddar cheese, pressing cheese
into mixture. Cover and refrigerate 8 hours. Serve with
your favorite dipping chip.

Black Lantern Resort and Retreat

Black Lantern Resort and Retreat

26844 320th Street • Shevlin
612-812-7309 • www.blacklanternretreat.com

A short drive from the headwaters
of the Mississippi and the lakeside
town of Bemidji, home to lumberjack
legend Paul Bunyan and Babe the
blue ox, is the Black Lantern Resort
and Retreat. The massive outdoor
venue hosts stunning events, and its
forested property provides secluded
lodging, a cabin built on stilts in the
canopy of the pines like a treehouse,
eight camping sites, a lake and ATV,
snowmobile and hiking trails. The
ultra private resort was designed
for individuals and groups to enjoy themselves and not be swamped by the masses.
Come and make memories on the 200 beautiful acres at a place built to last.

Hummus

2 garlic cloves, minced (divided)
1 (19-ounce) can garbanzo beans, half the liquid reserved
4 tablespoons lemon juice
2 tablespoons tahini
1 teaspoon salt
Pepper to taste
2 tablespoons olive oil

Place 1 clove minced garlic and beans in blender; process briefly, about 1 minute. Add lemon juice, tahini, additional minced garlic clove and salt in blender. Blend until creamy and well mixed.

Pour into medium serving bowl. Sprinkle with pepper and pour olive oil over the top. Serve with warm pita bread.

Minneapolis Greek Festival

Minneapolis Greek Festival

September

St. Mary's Greek Orthodox Church
3450 Irving Avenue South
Minneapolis
612-825-9595
www.mplsgreekfest.org

The mission of the Minneapolis Greek Festival is to share their culture with the community and raise funds for St. Mary's Greek Orthodox Church and a variety of programs and charities.

This 3 day festival shares Greek culture and food, overlooking the eastern shores of Lake Calhoun in Minneapolis. There are traditional dance performances, a 5k run, delicious Greek food, music, cooking demonstrations, wine tastings and children's activities.

Garlic-Cheese Spread

2 cups shredded American cheese
5 garlic cloves, minced
1 bell pepper, cored, seeded and chopped
1 (8-ounce) package cream cheese, softened
10 stuffed olives, finely chopped
1 celery stalk, finely chopped
1 tablespoon mayonnaise
1 teaspoon red pepper
⅓ bottle Worcestershire sauce
Salt to taste

Combine cheese, garlic and bell pepper. Add cream cheese, and blend well. Add olives and celery. Add mayonnaise, red pepper, Worcestershire and salt. Blend well and refrigerate. Serve with crackers.

Walnut Chicken Spread

1¾ cups chicken, cooked and chopped
1 cup finely chopped walnuts
⅔ cup mayonnaise
1 celery rib, finely chopped
1 small onion, finely chopped
1 teaspoon salt
½ teaspoon garlic powder

Combine all ingredients and thoroughly mix by hand. Serve with crackers.

St. Louis County Fair

Smoked Trout Paté

8 ounces cream cheese, softened
8 ounces smoked trout or salmon, chopped
1 clove garlic, finely minced
1 teaspoon lemon juice
1 teaspoon Worcestershire sauce

Combine all ingredients. Serve with favorite crackers. Other great additions are green onion, cayenne pepper, horseradish and dill.

National Trout Center
Preston Convention and Visitors Bureau

City of Preston

www.prestonmntourism.com
888-845-2100 • 507-765-2100

Get hooked on Preston! – "Minnesota's Trout Capital". Preston is a welcoming family-fun destination offering a variety of entertaining, educational and recreational activities. Visit the National Trout Center, go fishing in blue ribbon cold water streams, enjoy 60 miles of scenic paved bike trails in SE Minnesota's beautiful historic bluff country, take a naturalist led tour of the Mystery Cave (the longest cave in Minnesota), go back to a 19th century pioneer village with costumed guides at Historic Forestville, and canoe, kayak or tube along the Root River, also named one of the Top 10 Trout Waters by Outdoor Life Magazine, and experience Amish culture on a guided Amish tour. Nearby Forestville State Park offers camping, fishing and miles of cross-country ski, snowmobile and horseback riding trails. Preston's nationally acclaimed JailHouse Inn has been featured on the Today Show and Good Morning America. The city's annual Trout Days celebration is held the third weekend in May.

Fish Pond Salmon Spread

2 cups smoked salmon
2 tablespoons chopped onion
1 (8-ounce) package cream
   cheese, softened
1 tablespoon lemon juice
¼ cup sour cream
¼ cup mayonnaise
⅛ teaspoon dill weed
¼ teaspoon Worcestershire
2 tablespoons chopped capers

Finely chop salmon and combine with onion. Blend with all remaining ingredients except capers. Stir in capers and chill for several hours. Serve with crackers.

Douglas County Fair

Salmon Party Log

2 cups salmon
1 (8-ounce) package cream
   cheese, softened
1 tablespoon lemon juice
2 teaspoons grated onion
1 teaspoon prepared horseradish
¼ teaspoon salt
¼ teaspoon liquid smoke
½ cup chopped pecans
3 tablespoons snipped parsley

Drain and flake salmon, removing skin and bones. Combine salmon with next 6 ingredients; mix thoroughly. Chill several hours. Combine pecans and parsley. Shape salmon mixture in 8x2-inch log, roll in nut mixture. Chill well. Serve with crackers.

Tip:

Mix nuts and parsley on aluminum foil and roll it up to chill.

Margaret Chiglo
Stand Still Parade

Ham and Dill Pickle Appetizer Bites

Whole dill pickles
Thin deli ham slices
Cream cheese, softened

Cut dill pickles lengthwise into fourths or sixths, depending on how thick the pickles are. Dry with paper towel. Spread each ham slice with a very thin amount of cream cheese. Place dill pickle slice on edge of each ham slice. Trim ham if it is very much bigger than dill pickle spear. Roll up ham around pickle. Seal edge with cream cheese. Cut into 1-inch thick pieces. Arrange on plate and serve with toothpicks.

Wabasha Street Caves

Pickled Jalapeños

8 cups sliced jalapeños with seeds
8 cups chopped onion
½ cup salt
5 cups mild cider vinegar
5 cups sugar

Place jalapeños and onions in bowl. Pour salt on top; do not stir. Refrigerate 3 hours. Rinse well with cold water. Place vinegar and sugar in saucepan and heat to boiling. Add jalapeños and onion, stirring occasionally. Heat to scalding but not boiling. Place in hot jars and seal.

Sarah Yurcek
Younger Brothers Capture

Pepperoni Pizza Pita Pockets

1 package pita bread (pre-sliced in middle for sandwiches)
1 jar pizza sauce
1 package pepperoni
2 packages Italian shredded cheese

Open pita bread. Spread pizza sauce along inside edges. Line with pepperoni. Stuff center with Italian shredded cheese. Cook in oven at 425° for 10 minutes or wrap in foil and cook over fire.

Appeldoorn's Sunset Bay Resort

Roasted Pumpkin Seeds

Roasting pumpkin seeds is a great treat for Fall. They are fun to roast and a good source of protein, zinc and other vitamins.

Remove seeds from pumpkin. Separate and discard pulp. Thoroughly wash seeds in warm water. Spread seeds onto a cookie sheet. Sprinkle generously with salt.

Bake at 350° for 20 minutes. Check every 5 minutes and stir, adding more salt if desired. Check seeds for doneness by tasting. If insides are dry, they are done. Allow to cool and serve.

Variations - Replace salt in original recipe with the following suggestions:

Cheesy Pumpkin Seeds - sprinkle with cheesy popcorn seasoning.

Tex-Mex Style - Sprinkle powdered taco seasoning onto seeds. This is better mixed in a bowl first. Add more red pepper powder for a really hot seed!

Cajun style - Mix seeds in bowl with Cajun seasoning mix. For extra kick, add extra hot sauce.

Garlic Salt - yum!

Center Creek Orchard

Blue Cashew Truffles

2 tablespoons blue cheese, crumbled
2 tablespoons cream cheese, softened
1 tablespoon Italian parsley, finely chopped
1 tablespoon minced shallots
1 teaspoon ground white or black pepper
¼ cup whole cashews

Combine blue cheese, cream cheese, parsley, shallots and pepper in medium mixing bowl. Stir with fork until well mixed; set aside. Reserve 6 whole cashews. Place remaining cashews in food processor and chop until fine crumbs. Measure 6 tablespoons cheese mixture and form 6 little round logs. Roll each log in cashew crumbs and place 1 whole cashew on top. Refrigerate 1 hour. Makes 6 truffles.

Bonnie Deardorff
Deardorff Orchards and Vineyards

Deardorff Orchards and Vineyards

8350 Parley Lake Road • Waconia
952-442-1885 • www.DeardorffOrchards.com

Deardorff Orchards and Vineyards is a family farm nestled on 120 scenic acres, less than one hour west of Minneapolis. Visitors are invited to pick their own juicy apples from 4,000 trees.

Varieties include Honeycrisp, SweeTango, Zestar!, Haralson and many others. The gorgeous, century old barn has a gift store, apple tasting, cider bar, apples, jam, honey, pumpkins, mums, giftware and more. The farm is a fall destination for families, offering tractor/wagon rides out to the orchard for apple-picking, farm animals, kids' haystack and educational tours for young children.

Deardorff Orchards and Vineyards is also the home of Parley Lake Winery (see page 235).

Hockey Skins

6 small potatoes
½ cup vegetable oil
½ teaspoon salt

½ teaspoon pepper
½ teaspoon paprika or Cajun
seasoning

Preheat oven to 375°. Brush each potato lightly with oil and bake approximately 45 minutes. Cut potatoes in quarters lengthwise and scoop out centers, leaving about ¼-inch with skin. Combine salt, pepper and paprika in a bowl. Lightly brush inside of skins with oil and sprinkle with seasonings. Bake another 15 minutes or until browned to personal taste. Serve with toppings of your choice.

Amy Johnson
Tater Daze

Oriental Chicken Wings

30 chicken wings
1 cup soy sauce

1 cup brown sugar
1 cup butter

Wash chicken wings, discarding wing tips. Combine soy sauce, brown sugar and butter in saucepan over low heat. Arrange chicken in single layer in roaster. Pour sauce over chicken wings and bake uncovered at 350° for 1 hour, turning after 30 minutes. Lower temperature to 225°, cover and bake an additional hour, again turning after 30 minutes.

Char Johnson
Stand Still Parade

Party Sandwiches

6 bacon slices, cooked crispy
2 cups shredded Cheddar cheese
1 small onion
1 medium bell pepper, seeded and cored
½ cup pitted ripe olives
2 hard-boiled eggs
Pepper to taste
⅛ teaspoon garlic powder
¼ cup ketchup
1 tablespoon prepared mustard
10 hamburger buns, split

Place bacon, cheese, onion, bell pepper, olives and eggs into food processor and process till just coarse. Place in bowl. Add pepper, garlic powder, ketchup and mustard; mix well. Spoon mixture onto bottom halves of buns. Place on cookie sheet and broil until cheese melts, about 2 minutes. Top with tops of buns and cut in half.

Hot Island Russian Lullaby Tea

1 quart orange juice

1 quart pineapple juice

1 quart coconut juice

1 quart black or green tea

5 cinnamon sticks

2 tablespoons whole clove

2 tablespoons honey

Play your favorite music and bring everything to a soft boil in a large pot. Turn down heat, simmer for a time, then serve.

Terrapin Station
Muskie Days

Muskie Days Music Festival

July

"Meet me at the Muskie"
Nevis
www.nevischamber.com

For those interested in Muskies, they've got the world's largest right in the middle of the town! When visitors come to Nevis Muskie Days, they take part in a tradition that began in 1950 when carnivals were the rage. Nowadays, the carnival atmosphere continues with one of the best small town music festivals around. The Muskie Days Music Festival is a musician's and music lover's event, bringing together a wide range of original music from genres including Americana, Blues, Roots, Folk, Bluegrass and Jam music. Come and enjoy Nevis Muskie Days, and while you're there don't forget to take a picture in front of the World's Largest Muskie!

Rhubarb Slush

8 cups chopped rhubarb
8 cups water
3 cups sugar
1 (3-ounce) package strawberry Jell-O
¼ cup lemon juice
Lemon-lime soda

Cook rhubarb in water until soft. Add sugar and Jell-O. Stir until dissolved; strain. Add lemon juice. Store in ice cream pail and freeze. When ready to serve, combine 1 part lemon-lime soda and 1 part frozen slush mix.

Adeline Yates
Younger Brothers Capture

The Town of Nevis

Nevis is a small northern Minnesota town that brims with ambitious, and perhaps unusual, events throughout the summer including Nevis Muskie Days Music Festival, Pig Races, Uff Da Days, a successful Triathlon and more. The schedule of events is listed at www.nevischamber.com.

Coolers

8 cups watermelon cubes
1½ cups ginger ale
⅓ cup water
1 (6-ounce) can frozen limeade concentrate

Place watermelon cubes in a single layer in extra-large zip-lock bag. Freeze at least 8 hours. When ready to serve, remove from freezer and let stand at room temperature 15 minutes. Place half each watermelon, ginger ale, water and limeade in blender; process until smooth. Pour into pitcher, repeat with remaining ingredients. Serve immediately. Beautiful served with colored sugar crystals on rim of glass.

Variations:

Substitute honey dew for watermelon and use lemonade concentrate instead of limeade.

Substitute cantaloupe for watermelon, continue with limeade concentrate. Add 2 teaspoons fresh grated ginger to mixture.

Tall Timber Days

Raspberry Infusion Cocktail

1 ounce Raspberry Infusion
1 ounce Kettle One Vodka

Shake Raspberry Infusion and Vodka on ice. Decant into martini glass and garnish with frozen raspberries.

Saint Croix Vineyards

Saint Croix Vineyards

6428 Manning Avenue North • Stillwater
651-430-3310 • www.scvwines.com
www.facebook.com/saintcroixvineyards • twitter.com/SCV_Wines

Established in 1992, Saint Croix Vineyards has built a reputation for producing fine Minnesota wines. Their award-winning wines range from the dark, intense, oak-aged Marquette to the semi-dry La Crescent, reminiscent of a fine German Riesling. Their most memorable wine, Raspberry Infusion, is a decadent wine described by the Star Tribune as

"...a massive dessert wine that begs to be consumed with chocolate." Saint Croix Vineyards welcomes guests to visit their rustic tasting room in a century old barn, enjoy a stroll through their picturesque vineyards, and enjoy a picnic overlooking the quiet pond. Private tours are available by appointment only; a complimentary tour is offered each Saturday at Noon (12:00pm) April - November. Wine sampling is available during tasting room hours.

Champagne Punch

Fantastic punch for wedding receptions.

6 bottles dry champagne, chilled
3 bottles Sauvignon Blanc, chilled
3 pints brandy, chilled
3 quarts sparkling water, chilled

Pour in large punch bowl over ice block. Enjoy!

Punch for a Crowd

3 pounds sugar
2 quarts strong tea
2 dozen seedless oranges
4 dozen lemons

2 cans pineapple juice
12 quarts ginger ale, chilled
1 jar cherries
1 ice block

Dissolve sugar in tea while still hot. Cut oranges in half, reserving ½ of each. Squeeze juice from remaining orange halves and lemons into tea. Add pineapple juice. Chill. Add ginger ale when ready to serve. Drain cherries and add to punch. Slice reserved orange halves and add to punch with ice block.

Sweet and Spiced Coffee

3 cups prepared coffee
1 pint vanilla ice cream
1 cup whipped cream
3 tablespoons honey
½ cup rum
1 cup crushed ice

Pour hot coffee over ice cream. In separate bowl, add honey to whipped cream. Fold into coffee-ice cream mixture. Add rum and crushed ice.

Coffee Creamer

1 pint whipping cream
1 cup honey
⅓ cup sugar
1 tablespoon pure vanilla

Combine whipping cream and honey in saucepan over medium-low heat and stir until incorporated, about 1 minute. Add sugar and continue to stir until sugar dissolves. You do not want to boil this. Remove from heat; stir in vanilla. Pour into a jar and refrigerate!

Northland Woolens

Mocha Cooler

1 cup milk
¾ cup water
¼ cup half-and-half
1 tablespoon instant coffee
3 tablespoons chocolate malt powder
1 tablespoon sugar

Combine all ingredients in shaker. Serve over ice.

Wassail

2 quarts sweet apple cider
2 cups pineapple juice
1½ cups orange juice
¾ cup fresh lemon juice
1 cup sugar
2 cinnamon sticks
1 teaspoon whole cloves

Combine all ingredients in large saucepan. Heat over medium-high heat, bringing just to a boil. Reduce heat and simmer 20 to 30 minutes. Serve hot.

Soups, Salads & Breads

Wild Rice Soup

1 cup wild rice
½ pound bacon
3 tablespoons bacon drippings
¾ cup chopped celery
1 cup chopped onion
⅓ cup chopped green bell pepper
2 (14.5-ounce) cans chicken broth
1 (16-ounce) can mushroom pieces
3 (10.5-ounce) cans cream of
    mushroom soup

Rinse rice in cold water. Place rice in saucepan and cover with water.
Boil rice 15 minutes; drain. Fry bacon until crisp. Remove bacon and
crumble. Sauté vegetables in bacon drippings. Put vegetables in large
kettle. Add rice, chicken broth, mushrooms, mushroom soup and bacon.
Simmer 1 hour. Do not add salt.

Joan Ruen
Bluffscape Amish Tours

Chilly Day Wild Rice Soup

2 tablespoons butter
1 tablespoon minced onion
¼ cup flour
4 cups chicken broth
½ teaspoon salt
2 cups cooked wild rice
1 cup half & half
6 strips bacon, cut in small pieces
Minced chives and parsley
    (optional)

Sauté onion in butter until tender. Add flour then add broth gradually.
Stirring constantly, cook until mixture thickens slightly. Stir in salt and
rice. Simmer mixture approximately 5 minutes. Blend in half & half,
heating to serving temperature. Garnish with minced chives or parsley.

Glenwood Chamber of Commerce

Sally's Wild Rice Soup

1½ cups uncooked Minnesota wild rice
1 cup real butter
½ cup diced celery
1 cup chopped carrots
1 large yellow onion, chopped
2 cups sliced fresh mushrooms
2 tablespoons chicken bouillon base
1 tablespoon all-purpose seasoning
1 tablespoon pepper
1 tablespoon poultry seasoning
1 cup flour
1 (49.5-ounce) can chicken broth
4 pounds chicken, cooked and chopped
4 cups heavy whipping cream

Soak rice 8 hours; drain and rinse again. Cook according to package directions until fluffy and tender; do not overcook. Set aside. In a medium saucepan, melt butter and sauté vegetables until tender. Add bouillon base, seasonings and flour; cook 5 minutes. This will be very thick and hard to turn. Transfer to large kettle and add broth. Mix well until vegetable mixture is creamy. Add chicken and rice. Add heavy whipping cream; mix well. Cook 30 minutes over low heat. Serve hot.

Black Lantern Resort and Retreat

Minnesota Vacation Chicken Wild Rice Soup

3 cups chicken broth
½ cup flour dissolved in warm
   water
2 cups cooked Minnesota wild rice
1½ cups sliced mushrooms
1 cup cooked chicken, cubed

¼ cup wine
1 (12-ounce) can evaporated skim
   milk
Almond slivers (optional)
Salt and pepper to taste

In medium saucepan, heat chicken broth over medium-high heat. Stir in dissolved flour, wild rice, mushrooms and chicken, heating to a boil. Reduce heat and blend in wine and evaporated milk. Garnish with almond slivers, if desired. Season to taste with salt and pepper. Serve with toasted French bread slices.

Jodi Nies
Towering Pines Resort

Towering Pines Resort

35172 South Clamshell Drive
Pequot Lakes
218- 543-4738 • 800- 950-0267
www.toweringpines.com

Nestled among historic Minnesota pine trees, Towering Pines Resort borders the beautiful Clamshell Lake, part of the 14 interconnecting lakes of the famous Whitefish Chain of Lakes in Central Minnesota. Guests will enjoy wide, open, scenic lakefront access to non-motorized water equipment such as kayaks, fun bugs, hydrobikes, paddleboats and motorized rental boats. When not out on the lake, settle into one of the 19 fully furnished cabins designed for family comfort and relaxation. Listen to the calls of the Minnesota Loons, spot one of the many White-tailed deer snacking on apple trees, view many varieties of birds flying among the wooded walking trail or have a friendly competition on the 9-hole mini-golf course and family-friendly arcade. Gather friends and family for a fun Minnesota vacation!

Cabbage Soup

2 cups chopped celery
2 cups chopped onion
8 cups chopped cabbage
2 pounds kielbasa, sliced or chopped
1½ gallons ham stock
1 tablespoon garlic salt
1 teaspoon white pepper
2 cups dry non-dairy creamer
1 pound butter
3 cups flour
3 cups cooked diced potatoes

In large saucepot, combine celery, onions, cabbage, kielbasa, ham stock, garlic, salt and pepper. Bring to boil and simmer until vegetables are tender. Add non-dairy creamer. In small saucepot, melt butter and add flour until paste is formed. Cook over low heat 5 minutes, stirring constantly. Add to soup to thicken, and then add potatoes.

Executive Chef Terry Dox
Ruttger's Bay Lake Lodge

Tomato Basil Soup

2 tablespoons butter
¼ cup olive oil
4 carrots, peeled and finely minced
4 celery stalks, finely minced
2 sweet onions, finely minced
3 cans diced tomatoes
1 large can tomato juice
Pinch of sugar
½ cup chopped fresh basil leaves, divided
Salt and freshly ground black pepper to taste
Freshly grated Parmesan cheese

Heat butter and oil in a large, heavy, non-reactive pot. Add carrots, celery and onions and cook over medium-low heat 20 minutes or until soft. Do not brown. Add diced tomatoes, tomato juice, sugar and ¼ cup basil to vegetables and cook 15 to 20 minutes. Stir in remaining basil and season with salt and pepper. Serve immediately, topped with Parmesan cheese.

Joel Hays, owner
Bear Paw Resort

Broccoli Cheese Soup

2 cups sliced carrots
2 cups broccoli florets
1 cup diced celery
½ to 1 cup chopped onion
½ cup butter

¾ cup flour
10.5 ounces chicken broth
4 cups milk
1 pound Velveeta, cubed

In large saucepan, bring 2 quarts water to boil. Add carrots, broccoli and celery; cover and boil 5 minutes. Drain and set aside. In the same saucepan, sauté onion in butter. Add flour and stir to make a roux. Gradually add in chicken broth and milk. Cook until mixture thickens, 8 to 10 minutes. Add vegetables; heat until tender. Add cheese; heat until melted.

Jeanne Leksen
Stockyard Days

Stockyard Days

2nd weekend in August

Long Lake Regional Park
New Brighton
www.stockyarddays.org

New Brighton is a century-old city that is truly young at heart. This can easily be seen in the enthusiasm shown by the community volunteers at New Brighton's historic festival called Stockyard Days. The festival began in 1981 as a way to recall the early days of New Brighton as a center for the cattle industry including the stockyards, railroads, fashionable hotels and meatpacking plants.

Today, Stockyard Days is an 8 day event held throughout New Brighton. Area merchants, businesses and hundreds of volunteers participate in concerts, tournaments, a parade, street dances, a carnival, live entertainment, food sampling, fireworks, the finish line of the Antique Car Run, a car show, and the Miss New Brighton and Junior Ambassador Coronation. A medallion hunt is held, thousands of commemorative buttons are sold, prizes are raffled off, Goodwill Ambassadors are selected, and happy memories of times spent with family and friend are taken away.

"celebrating community"

Crockpot Beer Cheese Soup

1 can cream of mushroom soup
1 can cream of chicken soup
1 can cream of celery soup
2 cups water
2 beef bouillon cubes

1 tablespoon Worcestershire sauce
1 can beer (room temperature)
2 pounds Velveeta cheese, cubed
Dash Tabasco

Place all ingredients in slow cooker and cook on low 5 hours. Serve with popcorn or seasoned oyster crackers.

Bloomington Convention and Visitors Bureau

Brazilian Black Bean Soup

2 cups dry black beans
3½ cups beef stock
2 teaspoons salt

Cover beans with water and soak several hours. Drain beans. In saucepan, add beans, stock and salt; bring to boil. Cover and simmer 1½ hours over very low heat.

1 cup chopped onion
3 cloves garlic, crushed
1 large carrot, chopped
1 stalk celery, chopped
1 cup chopped green bell pepper
1 teaspoon ground coriander
1½ teaspoons ground cumin
2 tablespoons vegetable oil

Sauté onions and garlic. Add remaining ingredients and mix well. Add vegetable mixture to beans. Let soup continue to simmer over lowest possible heat.

Juice from 2 oranges
1 tablespoon white cooking wine
¼ teaspoon black pepper
¼ teaspoon red pepper
½ teaspoon fresh lemon juice

Combine squeezed orange juice, wine, black pepper, red pepper and lemon juice. Stir into soup. Cover and cook 10 minutes over very low heat. Adjust seasonings to taste. Serves 8.

Culturfest

Split Pea Soup
(Denmark)

2 cups split green peas
1 ham bone
1 stalk celery, chopped
1 large carrot, grated
1 small onion, chopped

¼ teaspoon thyme
¼ teaspoon cayenne
1 bay leaf
Salt and pepper to taste

Soak peas overnight in 1 quart cold water. Cover ham bone with water and cook 1 hour. Add peas and water to ham bone. Add remaining ingredients to soup. Boil hard 20 minutes. Reduce heat and simmer 1 hour. Remove ham bone; cut off meat and return to soup.

Culturfest

CulturFest

Garden Patch Soup

2 cups diced potatoes	2 teaspoons salt
2 cups diced carrots	½ teaspoon pepper
1 onion, chopped	1 pound ground beef
2 cups diced celery	1 egg
1 can tomatoes	½ tablespoon parsley
4 cups water	

Combine potatoes, carrots, onion, celery, tomatoes, water, salt and pepper in large pot. Simmer 30 minutes. Mix together ground beef, egg and parsley. Form into tiny balls and add to simmering soup. Continue cooking 20 minutes.

Culturfest

Culturfest

4th Saturday in September

Wilson Elementary School
325 Meadow Lane • Owatonna
507-451-3920
www.culturfest.org

Culturfest unites music and dance talents, sports, ethnic foods, authentic merchandise as well as children's and adult activities to enrich each visitor's experience. The festival invites food venders to sell their tantalizing ethnic cuisine from around the world. There are over 20 children's activity stations that are a part of the Passport Program. The children "take a trip around the world" while learning about various countries through hands-on activities. The students' passport gets stamped once they have finished each country's activity. The demonstration area gives visitors the chance to learn various crafts and ethnic skills from the far corners of the world. There are also a variety of artisans on hand to sell their wares. A wide variety of sports are played from rugby, cricket, soccer, parkour and much more. This is a great way for people to experience these sports up close.

Appeldoorn's Oyster Stew

2 tablespoons butter
1 clove garlic, sliced
2 green onions, chopped
½ teaspoon salt
½ teaspoon black or white pepper
1 pint oysters

1 cup whole milk
½ cup half & half cream
2 tablespoon chopped fresh parsley
Pinch of red pepper
Oyster crackers

Melt butter in skillet over medium heat. Add garlic, green onions, salt and pepper. Cook until fragrant. Add oysters with liquid and cook until edges curl. In a separate pan, heat milk and cream slowly. Pour oyster mixture into milk and cream. Add parsley and red pepper. Continue to heat, watching carefully so it does not scorch. Serve with crackers.

Appeldoorn's Sunset Bay Resort

Appeldoorn's Sunset Bay Resort

Pete's Reindeer Stew

Stew:

½ pound bacon, sliced

1½ tablespoons olive oil, divided

1 carrot, chopped

2 sticks celery, chopped

1 onion, chopped

2 cloves garlic, finely chopped

1½ pounds reindeer meat, cut into cubes (venison or beef can be substituted)

2 tablespoons flour

½ bottle red wine

1¾ cups game or beef stock

¾ cup sliced button mushrooms

1 bay leaf

Fry bacon in 1 tablespoon olive oil in a cast iron Dutch oven or other casserole suitable for stove tops. Add carrots, celery, onion and garlic. Cook gently until vegetables are softened. Remove vegetables and set aside. Coat reindeer, venison or beef cubes with flour. Add ½ tablespoon olive oil to skillet and increase heat. Brown meat on all sides. Add cooked vegetables, wine, stock, mushrooms and bay leaf to pan. Bring to a simmer. Prepare dumplings while stew is cooking.

Dumplings:

1½ cups self-rising flour

2 tablespoons fresh thyme, chopped

½ cup butter

Water

Place flour, thyme and butter into food processor and mix until consistency of fine breadcrumbs. Add a touch of water gradually until dough is firm but not too wet. Form dough into golf ball-sized dumplings and float them on top of stew. Cover and cook on a very low heat 1½ to 2 hours.

Detroit Lakes Polar Fest

Hunter's Stew

(Bigos)

This popular dish is a favorite at the festival and is considered the national dish of Poland.

2 tablespoons oil
1 large onion
3 teaspoons garlic powder
1 pound top sirloin or round steak
4 ounces cooked smoked ham, cut into 2-inch pieces
4 ounces smoked kielbasa or sausage, cut into 2-inch pieces
4 tablespoons flour
2 tablespoons mild paprika
2 cups chicken stock
2 cups beef stock
1 large can diced tomatoes
1 teaspoon marjoram
1 teaspoon thyme, chopped
1 teaspoon basil, chopped
1 teaspoon fennel
Salt and pepper to taste
1 head cabbage, grated
2 large apples, peeled, cored and diced
2 carrots, thinly sliced
1 small can mushrooms
8 to 10 prunes, chopped
½ cup wine (optional)

In large pot, heat oil over medium-high heat and sauté onion and garlic, cooking 2 to 3 minutes. Remove onion and set aside. Brown meat and add to onion; set aside. Sauté ham, cooking 2 to 3 minutes and add to meat and onion. Sauté kielbasa, cooking 2 to 3 minutes. Add meat, onion and ham back to pot. Sprinkle flour over mixture and cook until light brown. Add paprika and cook 1 to 2 minutes, stirring constantly. Gradually, pour in stock, add tomatoes and bring to boil. Reduce heat to simmer and add herbs, salt and pepper. Stir well, cover and cook over low heat 45 minutes. Stir occasionally and add more liquid if necessary (may add beef stock or water). Add cabbage, apples, carrots, mushrooms and prunes. Cook an additional 20 minutes. Add wine if desired. Cook another 10 minutes and serve. Delicious served with warm, crusty Polish rye bread.

Marie Przynski, Chief of Security
Twin Cities Polish Festival

Twin Cities Polish Festival

August

Old Main Street • Minneapolis
www.tcpolishfestival.org

Experience "All Things Polish"
at the Twin Cities Polish Festival.

Celebrate and explore the Polish heritage and culture that is a vibrant part of Minnesota. The tantalizing aroma of Polish sausage, pierogi and other traditional Polish cuisine, along with the melodies of traditional Polish songs, polkas, Chopin concertos and contemporary Polish music fill the air at this weekend event.

The Festival offers activities and entertainment for the entire family: Traditional folk art, music and dance; contemporary Polish artists; cultural exhibits; the Twin Cities Polish FilmFest; traditional Polish food and beer; Chopin celebration concerts; vodka tasting; rare Polish sheepdogs; children's area; music and entertainment on the polka and cultural stages from morning 'til night. Come early and stay late!

Crockpot Beef Stew

1½ pounds stew meat
¼ cup flour
1 teaspoon salt
½ teaspoon pepper
¾ cup beef broth
¾ jar Heinz mushroom gravy
1 medium onion, chopped

1 small garlic clove
1 teaspoon Worcestershire sauce
1 bay leaf
1 teaspoon paprika
4 carrots, sliced
3 diced potatoes

In a large bowl, combine stew meat, flour, salt and pepper coating meat well. Place meat mixture in large crockpot. Add remaining ingredients. Cook 5 to 6 hours on medium heat.

Cathy Kunze
Agate Days Celebration

He-Man's Stew

4 pounds stew meat
2 tablespoons oil
10 cups boiling water
Salt and pepper to taste
3 cups diced potatoes
1 small cabbage, chopped
2 rutabagas, diced

3 cups diced carrots
4 large onions, chopped
1 bag peas, frozen
2 cups diced celery
3 tablespoons beef bouillon
Kitchen Bouquet, as much as
   desired

Cut stew meat into ½-inch pieces. Brown on all sides with oil in Dutch oven. Add boiling water, salt and pepper. Bring to boil. Cover and simmer 1 hour. Sauté vegetables and add to Dutch oven. Add bouillon and Kitchen Bouquet and simmer stew 45 minutes or until vegetables are tender.

Culturfest

Crockpot Chili

2 pounds ground beef
1 cup chopped onion
1 green bell pepper, chopped
2 to 3 ribs celery, chopped
1 large (28-ounce) can crushed
  tomatoes
1 (8-ounce) can tomato sauce
2 cans kidney or pinto beans,
  drained
1 teaspoon pepper
3 teaspoons chili powder
Hot cayenne pepper to taste
1 teaspoon garlic

In a large skillet, brown ground beef and drain well. Combine
all ingredients in slow cooker, cover and cook 7 to 8 hours on
low, or until done.

Bloomington Convention and Visitors Bureau

White Chicken Chili

1 pound boneless, skinless chicken
  breast, cut into ½-inch pieces
1 medium onion, chopped
1 teaspoon garlic, chopped
1 tablespoon vegetable oil
2 (15½-ounce) cans great northern
  beans, rinsed and drained
1 (14½-ounce) can chicken broth
1 (4-ounce) can chopped green chilies
1 teaspoon salt
1 teaspoon ground cumin
1 teaspoon dried oregano
½ teaspoon pepper
¼ teaspoon cayenne pepper
1 cup sour cream
½ cup whipping cream

In a large saucepan, sauté chicken, onion and garlic in oil until chicken is no
longer pink. Add beans, broth, chilies and seasonings. Bring to a boil. Reduce
heat and simmer 30 minutes, uncovered. Remove from heat; add sour cream
and whipping cream. Serve immediately.

General Store Café Wild Rice Apple Salad

This recipe is naturally gluten free.

Dressing:

¼ cup white balsamic vinegar
2 tablespoons olive oil
2 small garlic cloves, minced
2 tablespoons honey

2 tablespoons Dijon mustard
1 tablespoon grated orange peel
Dash of salt

Salad:

2¾ cups cooked, chilled wild rice
   (available at the General Store of
   Minnetonka)
1¼ cups sliced celery

2 cups coarsely chopped red or
   green apple
2 tablespoons sunflower seeds
¼ cup Craisins

Whisk dressing ingredients together and pour over wild rice, celery, apples, Craisins and sunflower seeds. Toss together.

General Store of Minnetonka

General Store of Minnetonka

Monday-Friday 9:30-9:00 • Saturday 9:30-6:00 • Sunday 12:00-5:00

14401 Highway 7 • Minnetonka
952-935-7131 • www.generalstoreofminnetonka.com

Easy to find and definitely worth the trip, the General Store of Minnetonka is a 20,000 square-foot, locally owned and family operated business that was started in 1983. Upon entering the General Store, guests are greeted with an incredible selection of the latest in home décor, gifts, and so much more! A 2nd floor and Café were added in 2000 and recently

they have added a clothing boutique and an incredible jewelry selection. The General Store of Minnetonka features great brands such as: Pandora, Minnetonka Moccasins, Vera Bradley, Thymes, Caldrea and many more. This Lake Minnetonka landmark is a destination for those who crave something unique for themselves or for someone special. Stop by and see for yourself why the General Store of Minnetonka is a gift store like no other and a favorite of so many!

Wild Rice and Edamame Salad

½ cup blanched slivered almonds
2 tablespoons white sesame seeds
4 cups cooked wild rice
3 medium scallions, thinly sliced (white and light green parts only)
2 cups shelled cooked edamame, thawed if frozen
2 medium carrots, peeled and diced small
½ cup Craisins
3 tablespoons olive oil
2 tablespoons toasted sesame oil
¼ cup rice vinegar, plus more as needed
2 teaspoons honey
Kosher salt
Freshly ground black pepper

Place almonds in medium frying pan over medium heat and toast, stirring often until golden brown, about 8 to 10 minutes. Do not burn. Transfer to large heatproof bowl. Add sesame seeds to pan and toast, stirring often until golden brown, about 2 to 3 minutes. Transfer to bowl with almonds. Add rice, scallions, edamame, carrots and Craisins to almonds and sesame seeds; toss well. In a medium bowl, combine olive oil, sesame oil, rice vinegar, honey and a pinch of salt and pepper; whisk well. Drizzle over rice mixture and toss to combine. Taste and season as needed with more salt, pepper and vinegar. Cover and chill for 1 hour before serving.

Detroit Lakes Polar Fest

Dakota Day Wild Rice Salad

¼ cup finely chopped celery
3 green onions, thinly sliced
½ cup Craisins
½ cup dried blueberries
3 cups cooked wild rice, cooled

Mix celery, green onion, Craisins and blueberries into cooled rice.

Dressing:
¼ cup orange juice
½ cup vegetable oil

Combine orange juice and oil. Add dressing to rice mixture, toss and serve immediately

Gibbs Museum

Dakota Day

June

Gibbs Museum honors Jane's life-long friends by hosting a day of activities, games and food inspired by the Dakota. This salad was created to celebrate the annual fall wild rice migrations that brought Jane and her Dakota friends together each fall.

Spring Salad

Romaine lettuce or spring mix
   greens
Spinach
2 diced apples
Sunflower nuts

Red onion slices
Bacon Bits
Craisins
Bleu cheese crumbles (optional)

Combine all ingredients in a medium-size bowl. Refrigerate before serving

Poppy Seed Dressing:

1 teaspoon salt
¾ cup sugar
¾ cup vegetable oil

⅓ cup apple cider vinegar
1 tablespoon poppy seeds

Combine all dressing ingredients and mix well. Pour over green mixture right before serving.

Glenwood Chamber of Commerce

Detroit Lakes Polar Fest

February
Detroit Lakes
218-847-9202 • 800-542-3992
www.polarfestdl.com

Polar Fest is a ten-day winter celebration full of fun for the whole family. The events' mascot, Polar Pete, comes out of hibernation just to see the joy of winter on the faces of children and adults. After the festival, Pete returns to his den and slumbers deeply until summer comes and Detroit Lakes is alive with street faires, water carnivals, lake activities, outdoor theatre, and so much more. Which of these will you choose to do?

• Catch a prize-winning fish through an 8" hole in the ice.
• Holler "FORE" on a frozen lake after teeing off with your favorite driver.
• Take a brisk 5K run with a polar bear chasing you through the streets.
• Watch dads and their little sweethearts dance the night away.
• Plunge into the lake through the ice wearing a feather boa.
• Tailgate on a frozen beach and enjoy winter fireworks over a snowy lake.
• Don a bikini and winter boots, then dance and limbo in the sand to a beach band.

Fresh Green Salad with Almonds & Craisins

Topping:
1 cup slivered almonds
4 tablespoons sugar
½ cup Craisins
½ pound cooked bacon, crumbled

Heat small skillet over medium heat. Spray lightly with cooking spray, add slivered almonds and sugar. Stir constantly until almonds are toasted and candied, about 3 minutes. Watch carefully; do not scorch almonds. Mix candied almonds, Craisins and bacon together; set aside.

Dressing:
¼ cup sugar
⅓ cup vegetable oil
3 tablespoons red wine vinegar
¼ teaspoon salt
⅛ red onion, sliced into thin rings

Dissolve sugar with oil and vinegar. Add salt and onions; mix well.

Salad:
1 pound mixed greens
1 Granny Smith apple, cored and sliced
Blue cheese, crumbled

Toss greens with candied almond mixture. Add apple slices and crumbled blue cheese on top. Immediately before serving, pour dressing on mixed salad and toppings.

Detroit Lakes Polar Fest

Apple-Walnut Salad

¼ cup red wine vinegar
¼ cup fresh cranberries
2 tablespoons honey
1 tablespoon sugar
1 tablespoon red onion, chopped
¼ teaspoon salt
¼ teaspoon pepper
¾ cup canola oil
2 (5-ounce) packages spring mix salad greens
3 medium apples, sliced thin
1 cup chopped and toasted walnuts

Combine vinegar, cranberries, honey, sugar, onion, salt and pepper in blender until well mixed. While blending, gradually add oil. In large bowl, toss salad greens, apples and walnuts. Toss with vinaigrette from blender before serving.

Joan Ruen
Bluffscape Amish Tours

Apple-Romaine Salad

3 tablespoons fresh lemon juice
2 tablespoons honey
1 tablespoon grapeseed oil
1 teaspoon poppy seed
1 teaspoon onion flakes
Lemon pepper to taste
Fresh ground coarse sea salt to taste
4 cups torn romaine lettuce
1 cup coarsely chopped red apples
⅓ cup coarsely shredded carrots

In small bowl, combine lemon juice, honey, grapeseed oil, poppy seed, onion flakes, lemon pepper and salt; refrigerate until serving time. To serve, place lettuce in large salad bowl; top with apples and carrots. Toss with dressing.

Watkins Company
Visit Winona

Spinach Salad

Spinach or leaf lettuce
1 container bean sprouts
4 slices bacon, cooked and
    crumbled

4 ounces mushrooms
1 small can water chestnuts
1 small container feta cheese

Combine all ingredients in large bowl; toss well.

Dressing:

½ cup sugar
⅓ cup apple cider vinegar
½ cup canola oil

1 teaspoon paprika
1 tablespoon Worcestershire sauce
1 small onion, minced

Mix and pour over salad just before serving.

Albert Lea Convention and Visitors Bureau

The City of Albert Lea

507-373-2316 • 800-345-8414
www.albertleatourism.org

Albert Lea, known as "The Land Between the Lakes", has endless activities and events throughout the year. Shopping enthusiasts love the unique specialty gift and antique shops in the Historic Downtown area. There are over 40 parks, breathtaking wildlife and beauty along the Blazing Star Bike Trail which links to Myre Big Island State Park. The Freeborn County Historical Museum and Village is home to Marion Ross and Eddie Cochran memorabilia. Enjoy a scenic tour aboard the Pelican Breeze II Cruise Boat on beautiful Albert Lea Lake or tour Minnesota Nice Candle & Soap Factory. Take in a play, musical performance or Metropolitan Opera HD Live Stream at the Marion Ross Performing Arts Center.

Spectacular annual festivals include The Big Freeze, Land Between the Lakes Triathlon, Eddie Cochran Weekend,3rd of July Parade, Carnival, Car Show, 4th of July Fireworks, April Sorensen Memorial Half Marathon, BIB Barbeque, Strawberry and Fall Festival, Wind Down Wednesdays, Freeborn County Fair and the Big Island Rendezvous. For more information contact the Albert Lea Convention and Visitors Bureau. They are located at 102 West Clark Street, Monday through Friday 8am-5pm.

Taco Salad

1 pound coleslaw mix
1 to 3 green onions, chopped
2 cups shredded Cheddar cheese
1 large tomato, chopped
1 (16-ounce) bottle Western dressing
1 cup crushed Cool Ranch or Nacho Doritos

Combine first 4 ingredients. Just before serving add dressing and chips.

Wabasha Street Caves

Taco Salad

1 pound ground beef
1 package taco seasoning, reserve
 1 tablespoon for dressing
1 medium head lettuce
1 onion

2 cans kidney beans
3 cups shredded Cheddar cheese
⅓ cup sugar, divided
1 bottle Russian dressing
1 bag tortilla chips

Brown meat with taco seasoning (reserving 1 tablespoon); drain and cool. Place in bottom of large bowl. Cut lettuce fine. Dice onion very fine and mix with lettuce; place over meat. Drain and wash kidney beans and place over lettuce and onion mixture. Place cheese over lettuce and beans. Cover and refrigerate overnight. Mix remaining tablespoon taco seasoning and sugar with dressing. Crush tortilla chips and mix through meat, lettuce, kidney beans and cheese. Pour dressing over all.

Bloomington Convention and Visitors Bureau

Ramen Noodle Salad

1 package oriental ramen
1 package beef ramen
2 packages pre-packed coleslaw
5 to 7 green onions, chopped
¾ cup slivered almonds
1½ cups shelled sunflower seeds

Crush uncooked ramen noodles, reserve season packets for Dressing. Combine with remaining ingredients, tossing well.

Dressing:
1 cup sugar
½ cup apple cider vinegar
2 tablespoons soy sauce
1 tablespoon Worcestershire sauce
1 cup oil
Ramen season packets

Combine all ingredients, mixing well. Pour over salad. Tastes best when made the night before so it can marinate in the flavors.

Appeldoorn's Sunset Bay Resort

Chinese Coleslaw

4 to 5 cups Chinese cabbage, cut into bite-size pieces
1 cup shredded carrots
¼ cup chopped green onions
1 (8-ounce) can water chestnuts , drained and sliced
1 cup toasted slivered almonds
2 tablespoons toasted sesame seeds

In large bowl, toss together cabbage, carrots, onions and water chestnuts. Set aside while preparing dressing.

Dressing:
¼ cup oil
2 tablespoons sugar
1 tablespoon chopped fresh parsley
½ teaspoon salt
½ teaspoon ginger
Dash pepper
2 tablespoons vinegar
1 teaspoon soy sauce
Dash hot pepper sauce

In small bowl, combine all dressing ingredients; blend well. Pour dressing over vegetables; toss until well-coated. Cover; refrigerate 2 hours to blend flavors. Just before serving, add almonds and sesame seeds; toss to combine. Serves 10 to 12.

Culturfest

Minnes"O"ta Cucumber Salad

1 (7-ounce) box ring pasta
2 cup shredded cabbage
1 small sweet onion, diced

1 cucumber, diced
1 green bell pepper (seeded, cored and diced)

Cook pasta according to package directions, paying careful attention to not overcook. When pasta is almost done, drain in strainer and stir while rinsing with cold tap water. In large bowl, combine pasta with cabbage, onion, cucumber and bell pepper. Toss well and set aside.

Dressing:

1 cup sugar
1 cup light Miracle Whip

¼ cup vinegar
½ cup Marzetti coleslaw dressing

In small bowl, combine all ingredients and mix well. Add to pasta mixture. Refrigerate 24 hours. Stir well before serving.

Tracey L Hays, owner
Bear Paw Resort

Bleu Cheese Dressing

1½ gallons mayonnaise
2½ pounds sour cream
2½ pounds bleu cheese crumbles
1 tablespoon garlic powder
1 tablespoon onion powder
1 tablespoon Tabasco
2 tablespoons Worcestershire
1 quart buttermilk
½ cup shredded Parmesan

Combine all ingredients in a mixer and enjoy!
Yields 1½ gallons.

*Recipe Courtesy of Roasted Pear
Burnsville Convention and Visitors Bureau*

City of Burnsville

*12600 Nicollet Avenue Suite 100 • Burnsville
952-895-4690 • www.burnsvillemn.com*

For over two years, Burnsville has been chosen as a finalist for "Best for Food" in Rand McNally and in USA Today's Best of the Road® contest.

The Best of the Road® contest seeks the "Best Small Towns in America." Voters nominate towns in five different categories—Most Beautiful, Most Patriotic, Friendliest, Most Fun, and Best for Food. Burnsville was amongst 30 finalist towns, which are chosen by popular vote and editor's choice. Burnsville competed against 5 other towns for the ultimate title of "Best for Food."

Travel bloggers, The Road Bros, Mike Shubick and Brian Cox, spent a whirlwind 48 hours experiencing all Burnsville has to offer. The nominations speak for themselves... Burnsville is a beautiful town with friendly people, with tons of great food and fun things to do. On your journey through Minnesota, be sure to stop by, grab a bite and visit for a bit, you won't regret it.

Baby Corn Salad

2 cans baby corn, cut into ½-inch pieces
1 can French green beans, cut very small
1 red onion, finely chopped
1 red bell pepper, finely chopped

Combine all ingredients; set aside.

Dressing:
¾ cup canola oil, do not substitute
1 cup sugar
1 cup vinegar

Combine all ingredients, mixing until sugar is dissolved. Pour dressing over salad and toss well. Store in airtight container and refrigerate at least 48 hours before serving, mixing 4 times each day. Will last 2 weeks in refrigerator.

Black Lantern Resort and Retreat

Roller Coaster Potato Salad

4 pounds red potatoes, unpeeled, cooked, cooled and sliced
8 large eggs, boiled, peeled and sliced
2 cups Hellmann's salad dressing
2 tablespoons yellow mustard
¾ cup sugar
1 teaspoon salt
½ teaspoon white pepper
⅔ cup chopped onions
⅔ cup chopped celery
2 tablespoons horseradish

Combine all ingredients in large bowl. Mix well. Refrigerate at least two hours before serving.

Douglas County Fair

Tortellini Cranberry Salad

1 (18-ounce) package cheese-filled tortellini
1 (10-ounce) package dried cranberries
2 (3-ounce) packages dried bacon bits
1 to 2 bottles Poppy seed salad dressing
½ cup chopped green onions

Cook tortellini according to package directions. Combine all ingredients; toss well. Delicious served right away and will last 2 days in refrigerator.

Black Lantern Resort and Retreat

Pistachio Ambrosia Salad

2 (20-ounce) cans pineapple chunks
1 to 3 cups apple juice
4 (3.4-ounce) packages instant pistachio pudding mix
16 ounces sour cream
12 ounces prepared whipped topping
2 cups cubed fresh pears (canned, if out of season)
1 fresh orange, peeled and cut into bite-size pieces

Drain pineapple into large measuring cup and set aside pineapple chunks. Add apple juice to total 3 cups juice. Pour juice into 4-quart bowl. Add pudding mix and whisk until smooth. Stir in sour cream. Add whipped topping and mix until smooth. Fold in pineapples, pears and orange pieces. Chill several hours or overnight in serving bowl. Garnish with extra whipped topping, if desired.

Jodi Nies
Towering Pines Resort

Christmas Stewed Fruit

8 ounces large tapioca

8 ounces dried apricots, chopped

36 ounces pitted prunes

3 quarts water

30 ounces white raisins

16 ounces raisins

40 ounces purple grape juice

3 cups sugar

3 quarts apple cider

2 sticks cinnamon

Soak tapioca, apricots and prunes in water overnight. Combine all remaining ingredients and stir into prunes and apricots. Bake in large roaster at 325° for 3 to 4 hours. Stir occasionally until tapioca runs clear. Make 2 to 3 gallons. Good for several days refrigerated. Warm on stove; add water to thin.

Gibbs Museum

Pioneer Christmas

Second and Third Saturdays in December
Gibbs Museum, St. Paul

Costumed guides regale visitors with stories of Christmas past as they tour the soddy and farmhouse which is decked out for the holidays. Guests can create a cornhusk angel like the one atop the Gibbs family tree; visit baby animals in the barn; enjoy a stroll through the prairie where they can stop at the bonfire and enjoy a sip of hot chocolate and roast marshmallows. Staff creates a Gingerbread Victorian Village each year. Christmas stewed fruit is cooked and served in the farmhouse kitchen.

Apple Pineapple Salad

1 (20-ounce) can pineapple tidbits
¼ cup butter
2 tablespoons lemon juice
1 tablespoon cornstarch
2 tablespoons water

2 tablespoons sugar
2 cups unpeeled and diced apple
2 cups green grapes
2 teaspoons poppy seed
¼ cup chopped pecans

Drain pineapple juice into saucepan; set pineapple tidbits aside. Add butter and lemon juice and cook over medium heat until butter is melted. In small bowl, combine cornstarch and water until smooth; stir into juice mixture. Bring to a boil and stir 2 minutes. Add sugar. Cool to room temperature. In serving bowl, combine pineapple, apples, grapes and poppy seed. Add sauce and toss, coating well. Cover and chill for at least 1 hour. Just before serving gently toss in pecans.

Center Creek Orchard

Piña Colada Fruit Salad

1½ cups green grapes
1½ cups red grapes
1½ cups blueberries
1½ cups strawberries, halved

1 (8-ounce) can pineapple chunks,
   drained
½ cup raspberries

Wash fruit. Combine in bowl; set aside.

Dressing:
1 (10-ounce) can piña colada mix,
   thawed
½ cup sugar

½ cup pineapple-orange juice
⅛ teaspoon almond extract
⅛ teaspoon coconut extract

Combine all ingredients in bowl, whisking well. Pour over fruit mix and toss.

Hyde-A-Way Bay Resort

Carnival Popcorn Salad

1 cup mayonnaise
¾ cup sugar
½ cup chopped onion
1 can chopped water chestnuts
1 cup chopped celery
18 cups popped popcorn
1½ cups shredded Cheddar cheese
½ pound bacon, cooked and crumbled

Combine mayonnaise, sugar, onion, water chestnuts, and celery in a large bowl. Just before serving add the bacon, Cheddar cheese, and popcorn. Toss well and serve immediately.

Douglas County Fair

Douglas County Fair

3rd week in August

Douglas County Fairgrounds
Alexandria
320-760-1278
www.mndouglascofair.com

Alexandria is home to one of the largest county fairs in the state. Take exit 100 off of interstate 94, the fair grounds are just a short 4 miles north. The annual fair runs 4 days from Thursday through Sunday and draws approximately 45,000 visitors. Specific information about the fair is available on their website starting in June. It contains everything visitors need to know concerning entertainment, grandstand events such as the demolition derby, tractor pull and speedway racing, and gate information. Visit with over 100 different animals and learn about life on the farm by spending time in the 4-H barns. There are dozens of food vendors, clowns, a major carnival with thrilling rides and lots of fun children's activities. This is an event not to be missed. Make plans today to visit the beautiful Minnesota lakes area and attend this very special county fair.

Janet Bennett's Bumstead's

¼ pound American cheese, cut ½-inch cubes
1 can tuna fish, drained
3 eggs, boiled and chopped
2 tablespoons finely chopped onions (optional)
2 tablespoons finely chopped stuffed olives
3 tablespoons sweet pickle relish, drained
½ cup mayonnaise
10 hot dog buns

Preheat oven to 325°. In medium-size bowl combine cheese, tuna, eggs, onions, olives, relish and mayonnaise; mix well. Spoon into rolls, wrap each in foil and place on cookie sheet. Bake 25 minutes and serve. Makes 10 sandwiches.

Minnesota Boutiques

Cheesy Bread

Requires bread maker

¼ cup yellow cornmeal
½ cup boiling water
1 package dry yeast
½ cup warm water
¼ cup dark molasses

2 tablespoons butter
1 teaspoon salt
2½ to 3 cups flour
Cheddar cheese cubes

Mix cornmeal and boiling water, stir and let stand 1 minute. Add remaining ingredients, except cheese, to bread maker according to directions. Add cornmeal mixture. Set bread maker to dough setting. After dough cycle is over, put dough on counter and push in cheese cubes. Seal bottom. Allow to rise ½ hour. Bake at 350° for 30 minutes in 9-inch pie pan.

Julie Youngren
Agate Days Celebration

Popovers

4 eggs, slightly beaten
2 cups milk
2 cups flour
1 teaspoon salt

Preheat oven to 450°. Grease 12 muffin cups. Combine all ingredients and stir until smooth. Do not over mix. Fill cups almost full. Bake 20 minutes. Cut tops open and bake 5 more minutes.

Hyde-A-Way Bay Resort

Pleasin' Popovers

6 eggs, slightly beaten
1 cup milk
¼ cup salad oil
½ teaspoon salt
1 cup flour

Preheat oven to 450°. Using an electric mixer, whip eggs, milk, and salad oil together. Add salt and flour; mix on medium speed until smooth. Heat empty popover pans 5 minutes in oven. Remove heated pan and fill ¾ full. Bake 30 minutes. Reduce heat to 300° and cook additional 15 minutes. Do not open oven door while baking.

A maze'n Farmyard

Baking Powder Biscuits

2 cups flour
1 tablespoon baking powder
½ teaspoon salt

⅓ cup cold butter, sliced
¾ cup buttermilk

Combine flour, baking powder and salt in a bowl. Cut in butter. Add buttermilk, stirring until mixture forms slight ball shape. Knead gently on lightly-floured surface until workable dough forms. Press or roll ¾-inch thick and cut into 12 squares using a pizza cutter. Place biscuits on ungreased baking sheet and bake at 450° for 10 to 12 minutes or until golden. Serve hot! Yield: 1 dozen.

Wabasha Street Caves

Wabasha Street Caves

215 Wabasha Street South • St. Paul
651-224-1191
www.wabashastreetcaves.com

Cave tours: Thursdays at 5pm, Saturdays at 11am, Sundays at 11am year round

Gangster Tours: Saturdays at noon year round

Wabasha Street Caves is an event facility that does many weddings, corporate parties, class reunions and other group gatherings. These are actual caves that were transformed into a 1930's nightclub called the "Castle Royal". Gangsters and Socialites would come to wine and dine in the unique ambiance. There are several tours available, beginning with a tour company called "Down In History" which incorporates history and entertainment. There is also a Historic Cave Tour and several bus tours including the Saint Paul Gangster Tour as well as the Ghost & Graves Tour, No Blarney Tour, Uff Dah! Tour, and Twin Town Tacky Tour. The on-site coffee shop is called Grumpy Steve's, serving its own original blends.

Honey Wheat Bread

¾ cup sugar (½ brown sugar / ½ half white sugar)
4¾ cups white flour, divided
1 teaspoon salt
3 cups warm water
2 teaspoons yeast
2 to 4 teaspoons honey
¾ cup vegetable oil
4 cups wheat flour

Mix together sugar, ¾ cup white flour and salt. Add warm water and yeast. Let stand until it rises a bit, then add honey and oil. Mix well. Add wheat and remaining 4 cups white flour. Let rise 30 minutes; punch down. 30 minutes later shape in loaves and let rise to double. Bake at 350° for 20 to 25 minutes. Makes 4 loaves.

Amish Tours of Harmony

Limpa
(Swedish Rye Bread)

2 cakes compressed yeast
1½ cups water, divided
1 cup sugar, divided
½ cup shortening
½ cup molasses

1 teaspoon baking soda
4 cups buttermilk
6 cups rye flour
3 tablespoons salt
8 cups white flour

Dissolve yeast in ½ cup water; add 1 teaspoon sugar. Combine remaining sugar, shortening, molasses and remaining water and bring to boil. In separate bowl, add baking soda to buttermilk, and mix well. Add hot liquid mixture to buttermilk mixture. Add yeast when liquid is lukewarm. Add rye flour and salt. Beat thoroughly. Add white flour gradually to make stiff dough. Knead well and place in greased bowl to rise until light; knead down once and when light, shape into 6 round loaves. Place on greased tins and let rise until light. Bake at 375° for 45 minutes.

Culturfest

Minnesota Blueberry Muffins

Crumble Topping:
½ cup sugar
¼ cup butter, softened
1½ teaspoons cinnamon

Using a pastry blender, cut together sugar, butter and cinnamon; set aside.

Batter:
1 cup frozen or fresh blueberries
2 tablespoons sugar
1¾ cups flour
¼ cup sugar
2 teaspoons baking powder
1 egg
¾ cup milk
⅓ cup oil

Preheat oven to 400°. Line standard muffin tin with paper liners. Combine blueberries and sugar, toss well and set aside. In separate, large mixing bowl, combine flour, sugar and baking powder; set aside. In separate bowl, combine egg, milk and oil with fork. Add wet ingredients to dry ingredients and stir until moistened. It is okay to leave lumps, too much stirring will make a dense muffin. Gently fold blueberries into batter. Fill muffin cups with ⅔ cup batter. Sprinkle crumble topping over top of each cup. Bake 20 to 25 minutes or until golden. Test for doneness when inserted toothpick comes out clean.

Jodi Nies
Towering Pines Resort

Orange Glazed Mini Muffins

A pale yellow batter baked with tiny poppy seeds, then drizzled with a vanilla and almond extract-infused orange glaze while still hot and fresh out of the oven.

Once cooled, the glaze provides a slight crunch from the raw sugar, which melts in your mouth as you devour the sweet and satisfying mini muffin.

1½ cups flour	9 tablespoons butter, melted
1¼ cups sugar	¾ cup milk
¾ teaspoon salt	1 teaspoon poppy seeds
¾ teaspoon baking powder	¾ teaspoon vanilla extract
2 eggs, whisked	¾ teaspoon almond extract

Preheat oven to 350°. Line mini muffin tins with paper liners. Combine flour, sugar, salt and baking powder in a medium bowl; set aside. In a separate, large bowl, beat together eggs, butter, milk, poppy seeds, vanilla extract and almond extract for 2 minutes. Add dry ingredients to wet ingredients in 3 batches, mixing well between each batch. Fill each mini muffin cup half way with batter and bake 10 to 12 minutes, or until a toothpick inserted into the center comes out clean.

Glaze:

¼ cup fresh orange juice	½ teaspoon vanilla extract
¾ cup sugar	½ teaspoon almond extract

While muffins are baking, whisk together orange juice, sugar and extracts in a small bowl. Remove muffins from oven and drizzle ½ teaspoon glaze over each muffin while hot. Allow muffins to cool in tins before removing.

Dick Dahlen
Big Island Rendezvous

Pecan Pie Mini Muffins

1 cup packed brown sugar
½ cup flour
1 cup chopped pecans

⅔ cup butter, melted (no substitutes)
2 eggs, beaten

Combine brown sugar, flour and pecans, and mix well; set aside. In a separate bowl, combine butter and eggs. Stir into the flour mixture. Grease and flour miniature muffin cups and fill ⅔ full with batter. Bake at 350° for 20 to 25 minutes or until a toothpick inserted in center comes out clean. Remove immediately and cool on wire rack. Yields 2½ dozen.

Linda Kaeding
Agate Days Celebration

Agate Days Celebration

July

Moose Lake, MN
1-800-635-3680 or 218-485-4145
www.mooselakechamber.com

This infamous, fun filled weekend holds something for everyone with the Gem and Mineral Show at Moose Lake High School and Clark-Olsen Agate Stampede. During this event, 500 pounds of agates and $400 in quarters are strewn down Elm Avenue for spectators to collect with free admission! There is an agate and gem slide presentation at the Library Center prior to the stampede to help visitors identify an agate. There are tons of additional events throughout the weekend including Art in the Park featuring Bluegrass Jam, open gravel pits for agate picking, Fireman's Steak Fry, Sunday Entertainment in the City Park, and so much more.

Sponsored by the Moose Lake Area Chamber of Commerce and Carlton County Gem and Mineral Club

Corn Muffins

1 cup fine-ground whole-grain yellow cornmeal
2 cups flour
1½ teaspoons baking powder
1 teaspoon baking soda
½ teaspoon salt
2 large eggs
¾ cup sugar
1 stick unsalted butter, melted
⅔ cup sour cream
½ cup milk

Preheat oven to 400° with rack in middle position. Spray standard muffin tin with non-stick spray. With wire whip, mix cornmeal, flour, baking powder, baking soda and salt in medium bowl; set aside. Whisk eggs. Add sugar to eggs, whisking until thick, about 30 seconds. Add butter in 3 additions, whisking to combine after each addition. Add half the sour cream and milk, and whisk to combine. Add remaining sour cream and milk and whisk to combine. Add wet ingredients to dry. Mix with rubber spatula until batter is just combined and evenly moistened. Do not over mix. Using an ice cream scoop, divide batter evenly in 12-cup muffin pan. Bake 16 to 18 minutes, until muffins are lightly golden brown. Cool 5 minutes and invert onto wire rack. Serves 12.

Executive Chef Terry Dox
Ruttger's Bay Lake Lodge

Zucchini Bread

3 eggs
2 cups sugar
2 teaspoons vanilla
¾ cup vegetable oil
2 cups grated zucchini
1 (8-ounce) can crushed
    pineapple, drained
2 teaspoons baking soda

1 teaspoon salt
½ teaspoon baking powder
½ teaspoon cinnamon
¾ teaspoon nutmeg
1 cup walnuts
3 cups flour
1 cup raisins

Cream eggs and sugar; add vanilla and oil. Mix until foamy. Add zucchini and pineapple and mix well, stirring with spoon by hand. Add baking soda, salt, baking powder, cinnamon, nutmeg, walnuts, flour and raisins, continuing to stir with spoon. Bake at 350° for 1 hour. Makes 2 big loaves.

Culturfest

Banana Bread

½ cup butter, softened
1 cup sugar
1 teaspoon vanilla
2 eggs, beaten

1 teaspoon baking soda
3 tablespoons hot water
2 cups flour, divided
3 bananas, mashed

Cream together butter, sugar, vanilla and eggs. Dissolve baking soda in hot water and add 1 cup flour. Add bananas and remaining flour. Bake at 375° for 45 minutes. Freezes well.

Culturfest

Lemon Poppy Seed Bread

1 package lemon cake mix
1 package instant lemon pudding
4 eggs
1 cup hot water
½ cup cooking oil
¼ cup poppy seeds

Mix all ingredients together. Beat 4 minutes. Turn into greased and floured pans (3 regular or 5 baby loaves). Bake at 300° for 20 minutes, then at 325° for another 20 minutes. Inserted toothpick coming out clean ensures it is done.

Appeldoorn's Sunset Bay Resort

Kahlúa Bread

1 box yellow cake mix (with or without pudding)
1 large box instant chocolate pudding
4 eggs
1 cup oil
¾ cup water
¼ cup Kahlúa
¼ cup vodka
½ cup sugar

Combine all ingredients, mix will thicken. Pour batter into greased loaf pans. Bake at 350° for 45 to 50 minutes or until toothpick comes out clean.

Kristie Swenson
Trimont Fun Fest

Hibernation Fry Bread

3 cups flour
1 tablespoon baking powder
1 teaspoon salt

1¼ cups warm water
Extra flour for processing

To make dough, thoroughly blend flour with baking powder and salt in a mixing bowl. Make a well in the center of flour mixture and pour warm water in center of the well. Work flour mixture into water with a wooden spoon or use hands. Gently knead dough into a ball and form into a roll about 3-inches in diameter. Cover dough with a clean kitchen towel to prevent drying and let it relax 10 minutes. (This dough is best used within a few hours; it may be used the next day if covered tightly with plastic wrap, refrigerated and then allowed to warm to room temperature.)

To form bread, place dough on a cutting board. Cut dough with a dough cutter or knife into desired thickness. Cut into smaller pieces for appetizers and larger pieces for sandwiches. Begin cutting in center of roll and continue halving until all portions have been sliced. Cover pieces with a dry, clean towel while slicing to prevent drying. Place flour in a shallow pan to work with when rolling out dough. Lightly dust each piece place on a lightly floured work surface. With a rolling pin, roll each piece to about ¼-inch thickness. Place each finished piece in flour, turn and lightly coat each piece, gently shaking to remove excess flour. Stack rolled pieces on a plate as you move along. Cover with a dry towel until ready to cook.

Pour frying oil in a deep, heavy pan at least 1-inch deep. Place in oil. Do not overcrowd. Cook 2 to 3 minutes per side. This bread generally does not brown and should be dry on the exterior and moist in the center. Try cooking one piece first, let it cool, and taste for doneness. Place finished breads on a paper towel to absorb excess oil. Serve immediately.

Detroit Lakes Polar Fest

Soul Cakes

2 packets yeast
½ cup sugar, plus 1 teaspoon
¼ cup lukewarm water
¼ pound butter, softened
2 cups milk, scalded and slightly
   cooled

1 cup currants
6 cups flour
1 teaspoon salt
3 teaspoons cinnamon
½ teaspoon allspice
1 egg, beaten

Dissolve yeast with 1 teaspoon sugar in lukewarm water and let stand in warm place. Cream together butter with ½ cup sugar. Add milk and yeast, stirring well. Add currants. Sift flour, salt and cinnamon together and add to mixture, kneading for a few minutes and adding additional flour if needed. Place in bowl and place in warm spot. Let rise until doubled, about 1½ hours. Punch down. Shape dough into round buns and place in greased pan with buns touching. Let rise another 15 minutes. Brush beaten egg onto tops of buns with pastry brush. Bake at 375° for 15 to 20 minutes or until lightly browned. Yields 30 buns.

Gibbs Museum

Gibbs Museum of Pioneer and Dakota Life

2097 West Larpenteur Avenue • St. Paul
651-646-8628 • www.rchs.com

Gibbs Museum explores 19th-century pioneer and Dakota Indian life through the eyes of Jane Gibbs. Jane and husband Heman arrived in the newly formed Minnesota Territory in 1849 and raised a family of five while farming on the edge of St. Paul. However, Jane had grown up amongst the Dakota in the 1830s; the wild ricing trail crossing the Gibbs property reunited Jane with her childhood friends each fall. The Gibbs historic site boasts the original farmhouse built between 1854-1873, barns, replica sod house, one-room schoolhouse, Dakota summer bark lodge and several tipi.

Swedish Almond Toast

1 cup butter, softened	3½ cups flour
2 cups sugar	½ teaspoon salt
2 eggs	1 cup chopped almonds
1 cup sour cream	20 cardamom seeds, crushed

Cream together butter and sugar. Add eggs and beat well. Add sour cream and blend in flour and salt. Add nuts and cardamom seeds. Press dough into greased and floured 9x13-inch pan. Bake at 350° for 40 minutes. Cool and cut into ½-inch slices. Place slices upright and ½-inch apart on greased and floured baking sheet. Bake at 300° for 40 to 45 minutes or until slightly dry and lightly browned. Remove toasts from baking sheet. Cool completely on a wire rack, then store in a tightly covered container.

Sylvia Benson
Santa Lucia Festival

Santa Lucia Festival

December

Bemidji
877-250-5959

The Bemidji Santa Lucia Festival, begun in 1976, is held annually each December, beginning at 6:00am on a dark and frosty Northern Minnesota morning. In a darkened room between 150 and 300 people await the entrance of Santa Lucia, a young woman dressed in a white gown with a crown of glowing candles upon her head, leading attendants, star boys and others. Lucia represents the legend of a young maiden who brings food to the poor and starving. A program of traditional Scandinavian music and dance is followed by a smorgasbord of delicacies including Swedish meatballs, herring, and rice pudding. By 8:00am the Fest is over. Lucia, some of her attendants and tomtes (elves) leave the festival to visit a school or nursing home to entertain and share this tradition with the community.

Apple Pie Stuffed French Toast

Use large loaves of sandwich bread for this recipe, with slices about 5x4 inches. If using smaller, standard-sized sandwich bread, all filling will not be used.

4 ounces cream cheese, softened
1½ tablespoons sugar
3 tablespoons apple butter
¼ teaspoon ground cinnamon
8 slices good-quality sandwich bread
1 large egg
1 cup cold water
½ cup flour
1 teaspoon vanilla extract
4 tablespoons unsalted butter, divided
Maple syrup for serving

Combine cream cheese, sugar, apple butter and cinnamon in medium bowl. Spread on 4 bread slices. Top with remaining bread slices, pressing down gently, forming 4 sandwiches. Combine egg, water, flour and vanilla in shallow pie plate. Melt 2 tablespoons butter in large nonstick skillet over medium heat. Dip both sides of 2 sandwiches in batter and place in skillet. Cook until deep golden brown on both sides, about 3 minutes per side. Repeat with remaining butter and bread. Cut into triangles and serve immediately with maple syrup.

Center Creek Orchard

French Potato Pancakes

2 large potatoes, peeled and
   grated
1 medium onion, grated
2 tablespoons flour
2 teaspoons salt
Pepper

Nutmeg
½ teaspoon chopped parsley
2 egg yolks, slightly beaten
2 egg whites, stiffly beaten
1 tablespoon butter

Put potatoes and onion in medium bowl; add flour and seasonings; mix well. Add egg yolks and stir well. Fold in egg whites. Melt butter in skillet and add 2 tablespoons mixture for each cake. Cook over medium heat until golden brown on both sides.

Culturfest

Potato Pancakes

2 large eggs
1 teaspoon Kosher salt
¼ teaspoon pepper
2 pounds medium russet potatoes (3 to
   4), peeled and halved lengthwise

2 medium onions, quartered
½ cup matzo meal or breadcrumbs
4 tablespoons olive oil, divided
Applesauce

In a large bowl, whisk together eggs, salt and pepper. In a food processor fitted with a large grating disk, grate potatoes and onions. Add potatoes and onions to eggs and mix well. Add matzo meal and mix. Heat 2 tablespoons oil in a large skillet over medium heat. Gently drop 5 large spoonfuls of potato mixture onto skillet (about ¼ cup each). Spread out batter to create even pancakes and cook until browned, 4 to 6 minutes per side; transfer to plate. Repeat with remaining potato mixture, adding more oil to skillet as necessary. Serve with applesauce and sour cream.

Bloomington Convention and Visitors Bureau

Pumpkin Pancakes

2 cups biscuit mix
2 teaspoons cinnamon
¼ teaspoon ginger
¼ teaspoon nutmeg
2 eggs

1½ cups evaporated milk
¼ cup water
1 cup pumpkin
2 tablespoons vegetable oil
1 teaspoon vanilla

Combine all ingredients and mix well. Pour batter onto a hot griddle. Cook just until small bubbles form. Flip, and cook other side until golden. Serve warm.

Hyde-A-Way Bay Resort

Banana Pancakes

1 cup flour
2 tablespoons sugar
2 teaspoons baking powder
½ teaspoon salt
1 egg, lightly beaten

1 cup milk
2 tablespoons unsalted butter, melted
2 bananas, sliced into rounds

Whisk flour, sugar, baking powder and salt in medium bowl. Add egg, milk and butter; whisk until combined but still slightly lumpy. Heat a large nonstick skillet over medium heat. Place 5 banana rounds in pan, about 3 inches apart. Spoon 1 tablespoon batter over each; cook until large bubbles cover surface, 1 to 2 minutes. Flip, and cook until bottom is golden, about 1 minute more. Repeat with remaining banana rounds and batter.

Swedish Bacon Pancake

1 (12-ounce) package thick-sliced bacon
5 cups milk
3 eggs
3 cups flour

Lightly spray a large roasting pan with non-stick cooking spray. Remove as much of the excess white fat from the bacon as possible and discard. Chop bacon fine. Scatter across bottom of pan. Place on middle rack of cold oven and then preheat oven to 425°. Bacon should be cooked at the point oven reaches heat; if not, leave in a minute or two longer until crisped. Whisk together milk and eggs. Gradually add flour in ½-cup increments until well-blended. Once bacon is crisped, pour batter into pan. Whisk lightly to evenly distribute bacon. Return to oven and bake 25 to 30 minutes, until puffed and golden brown.

Serve with lingonberries as in Sweden or with maple syrup.

Karen Olson
Santa Lucia Festival

Lefse

This food was made during the depression from leftover potatoes after a meal, and it became a very popular treat. It is still a popular treat today.

6 cups cooked Russet potatoes, mashed	2 tablespoons powdered sugar
¼ stick butter	3 cups flour
3 tablespoons cream	Cinnamon and sugar to taste

Combine the first 5 ingredients; mix well. Form into small balls. On floured surface, roll each ball into patty so thin you can almost see through it. Using a Lefse stick*, place patties on 500° ungreased Lefse griddle.* Cook 3 to 5 minutes on each side. Using Lefse stick, remove from griddle, fold in half and place inside a dish towel to prevent drying out. When cooled, brush off excess flour, spread with butter and sprinkle with cinnamon and sugar.

*Lefse sticks and griddles can be found at most L&M Supply stores, and at Norwegian Import Specialty Shops.

Karen Pender, Director
St. Louis County Fair Board

St. Louis County Fair

July

Chisholm
www.stlofair.org

Every July the Midway comes to life with a traditional, American fair. Thousands of visitors come to eat delicious corndogs, funnel cakes, beef kabobs, cinnamon rolls and countless variations of lemonade, soda and ice cream. The livestock competitions draw people from all over the state, and the musical performances are not to be missed. Thrill seekers will find their fun with slides and rides with loops, flips and dips. Be sure to visit the website for yearly dates, admission and ticket prices, lodging and more.

Bucky's Lefse

6½ cups water
1 tablespoon salt
1 stick margarine
1 cup half-and-half
1 (15-ounce) box Hungry Jack instant potatoes
3½ cups flour

Bring water to boil. Add salt and margarine; stir until melted. Add half-and-half and remove from heat. Stir in instant potatoes; mix well. Refrigerate overnight. Using hands, mix 1¾ cup flour into ½ potato mixture. Make 2½-inch balls and roll out thinly on lefse board covered with a pastry cloth that is well floured. Keep dough chilled at all times for ease in rolling, keeping dough you are not working with in the refrigerator. Heat lefse griddle to 500° and cook until lightly browned. Flip with lefse stick and cook until lightly browned. Set cooked lefse aside covered with towel until completely cooled. Repeat with remaining dough. Serve with butter and sprinkle with brown sugar or cinnamon sugar.

Bucky Rogers
Stand Still Parade

Vegetables & Other Side Dishes

Garlic Roasted Asparagus

2 pounds asparagus, rinsed and dried
3 tablespoons olive oil
1½ tablespoons minced garlic
Salt
Pepper
2 teaspoons lemon juice

Preheat oven to 425°. In large glass baking dish, toss asparagus with olive oil and garlic; season with salt and pepper. Bake 15 to 20 minutes, until asparagus is tender and lightly browned, stirring twice. Remove from oven and toss with lemon juice.

A maze'n Farmyard

A maze'n Farmyard

57649 State Highway 55 • Eden Valley
320- 453-6901
www.amazenfarmyard.com

A maze'n Farmyard is a family affordable, fun destination. This fantastic family run business is located in central Minnesota. Since 2004, many families have been entertained and the Farmyard prides itself on having something for every family member! Included in the admission price is the hands-on animal petting farm, 9 holes of miniature golf, a giant slide, maze, pony rides, train rides, corn pit, bounce barn with 5 inflatable bouncers and parakeet barn. They are open daily from Memorial Day to Labor Day and weekends only in September and October.

Asparagus, Mushroom and Gorgonzola Risotto

1 small onion, chopped
5 tablespoons unsalted butter, divided
Salt to taste
1 cup Italian Arborio rice
1½ cups white wine, divided
½ to ¾ cup chicken broth
1 bunch thin asparagus, chopped (¾- inch pieces, hard portion
   removed)
¾ cup chopped cremini mushrooms
¼ pound gorgonzola
½ cup shelled and toasted hazelnuts

Sauté onion and salt in 3 tablespoons butter for 8 to 10 minutes. Add rice and sauté an additional 2 to 3 minutes. Add ½ cup wine and simmer until moisture is absorbed. Add chicken broth and allow to be absorbed. Add asparagus and mushrooms with additional ½ cup wine. Allow this to absorb prior to adding remaining wine and crumbled gorgonzola. Simmer until most of the moisture is absorbed and cheese is melted. Top with toasted hazelnuts.

Parley Lake Winery

Stuffed Mushrooms

24 large mushrooms
6 tablespoons vegetable oil, divided
3 tablespoons chopped onion
½ clove garlic, chopped fine
3 tablespoons chopped fresh parsley
Salt and pepper to taste
Fine breadcrumbs

Preheat oven to 375°. Wash mushrooms and remove stems. Chop stems and set aside. Place caps upside down in skillet with 2 tablespoons oil and sauté gently until light brown. Remove caps and set aside. Place remaining oil in skillet. Add chopped stems, onion, garlic, parsley, salt and pepper. Add enough breadcrumbs to make a thick stuffing. Fill each cap with stuffing and bake 20 minutes.

Tater Tot Hot Dish

1 pound hamburger
1 envelope onion soup mix
1 can chili beans, undrained
1 can diced tomatoes, undrained
1 can whole kernel corn, undrained
1 envelope taco seasoning
1 package frozen tater tots

Preheat oven to 350°. Brown hamburger and onion soup mix; drain. Stir in beans, tomatoes, corn and taco seasoning. Place tater tots on top. Bake 45 minutes.

Culturfest

Baked Breakfast Hash Browns

½ tablespoon butter
1 can cream of chicken soup
1 pint sour cream
½ cup milk
½ cup chopped green onions
2 pounds frozen shredded hash browns
2 cups shredded Cheddar cheese
1 cup crushed corn flakes

Preheat oven to 350°. Melt butter in 9x13-inch pan. Mix soup, sour cream, milk and onion together. Layer in pan, ½ hash browns, ½ soup mixture and 1 cup cheese; repeat. Top with crushed corn flakes. Bake 1 hour.

Dan and Mryna Gajeski
Tater Daze

Buttered Corn Days Parade in Sleepy Eye

Max's Potatoes

3 pounds new potatoes, boiled with skin
1½ cups butter, divided
2 teaspoons curry powder
2 teaspoons mustard seed
2 cups chopped green onions

Cube potatoes and brown in ½ cup butter. Melt remaining butter; add curry powder and mustard seed. Add to potatoes and toss, coating well. Immediately before serving, add green onions.

Myrna Scott, 1st prize, Hot Dish Category, 1984

Tater Daze

Farmers Market

www.brooklynpark.org/farmersmarket

Brooklyn Park has a thriving farmers market with opportunities to pick up fresh locally grown fruits and vegetables as well as flowers, jams, honey, bread, ice cream, crafts and much more. The market runs June through October, every Wednesday, 3:00-7:00pm.

Potatoes with Leeks

4 tablespoons butter
½ cup flour
2 cups whipping cream
6 cups sliced potatoes

3 to 4 leeks, thinly sliced
1½ teaspoons salt
1½ cups Swiss cheese

Melt butter. Add flour and gradually stir in whipping cream. Cook over medium heat until thickened. Mix with potatoes and leeks; add salt. Pour in a 9x13-inch pan and bake 1½ hours at 350°. Top with cheese and bake another 5 minutes.

Mayor Steve and Kathy Lampi
Tater Daze

Tater Daze

June

Noble Sports Park • Brooklyn Park
763-493-8013
www.taterdaze.org

Brooklyn Park's Tater Daze is a unique festival where residents pay homage to the humble potato. Early settlers discovered that potatoes flourished in the flat, sandy soil of the area. Throughout the Great Depression, drought and urbanization, Brooklyn Park has shown its strength as a community willing to work together and make our city a welcoming place for everyone.

When the festival started in 1965, nearly 40 growers cultivated almost 3,000 acres of potatoes. As Brooklyn Park has grown to the sixth largest city in Minnesota, Tater Daze has been a bridge to their heritage and a catalyst to connecting and celebrating this beautifully diverse community.

Tater Daze has fun activities for all ages including a parade, a business and craft fair, food, live music and performers, sports, contests, games and prizes. Tater Daze is a shining example of a thriving community inspiring pride where opportunities exist for all.

Rosemary Roman Potatoes

1½ pounds potatoes, cooked, chilled and cubed with skin on
¾ cup butter, melted
1 tablespoon garlic, chopped in oil
¾ to 1 cup Parmesan cheese, grated
Salt and pepper to taste
2 tablespoons fresh rosemary, minced

Fill deep fryer with enough oil to cover potatoes. Preheat oil to 350°.
Deep fry potatoes 2 to 3 minutes, until golden brown and crispy.
Remove potatoes and drain. Transfer to stainless steel mixing bowl.
Quickly add butter, garlic, Parmesan, salt and pepper. Toss, coating
thoroughly. Garnish with fresh rosemary.

Spirit Lake Steakhouse

Spirit Lake Steakhouse

185 North Main Street • Wahkon
320-495-3600 • www.spiritlakesteakhouse.com

Hours of Operation: Monday - Sunday 11:00 a.m. - 10:00 p.m.

Spirit Lake Steakhouse located on Main Street in Wahkon may be new to the area but has
found deep rooted meaning in this charming towns history. Located on the South side of
Lake Mille Lacs, Wahkon was one of the first known settlements on the lake in the late

1800's. Native Americans of the Dakota
tribe had a village here and referred to
Lake Mille Lacs as "mde wakan" meaning
"Spiritual Lake". This piece of unique
history was the inspiration when naming
Spirit Lake Steakhouse. While renovating
this historical building a great effort was
put in to maintaining its character. Come
and enjoy a chef inspired meal on the wood
fired grille or sip on a glass of wine. The
diverse menu offers a little bit for everyone.

Scalloped Potatoes

1½ cups milk
1 tablespoon flour
9 potatoes, peeled and sliced
Salt and pepper to taste
1 onion, sliced
2 cups chopped ham
1 (12-ounce) package shredded Cheddar cheese

Mix milk and flour. In slow cooker, layer potatoes, salt and pepper, onion, ham, cheese and milk mixture; repeat. Add a little extra milk, if needed, to almost cover potatoes. Cook on high 2 to 3 hours, stirring occasionally.

Culturfest

Cheesy Potato Slices

¾ cup dairy sour cream
5 or 6 medium potatoes, peeled
1 teaspoon salt
¼ teaspoon pepper
½ teaspoon seasoned salt
1 cup grated sharp Cheddar cheese
1 cup crushed wheat cereal

Spread sour cream evenly over bottom of 15x10-inch jelly roll pan. Cut potatoes crosswise into ⅓-inch thick slices. Place slices in single layer over sour cream. Turn slices, coating both sides. Sprinkle with combined seasonings then with cheese. Top with crushed cereal. Bake at 350° for 35 to 40 minutes or until slices are tender.

Appeldoorn's Sunset Bay Resort

Do-Ahead Garlic Mashed Potatoes

3 pounds red or white potatoes, peeled and cubed
6 cloves garlic, peeled
¾ cup milk
½ cup heavy cream
½ cup butter
1 teaspoon salt
Dash of pepper

Place potatoes and garlic in saucepan; add enough water to cover. Heat to boiling; reduce heat. Cover and cook 20 to 25 minutes or until potatoes are tender. Drain and return to saucepan. Heat potatoes over low heat about 1 minute to dry potatoes. Mash potatoes and garlic in pan until no lumps remain. Heat milk, whipping cream, butter, salt and pepper until butter is melted; reserve and refrigerate ¼ cup mixture. Add remaining milk mixture in small amounts to potatoes, mashing after each addition, until potatoes are light and fluffy. Spray 2 quart casserole with cooking spray. Spoon potatoes into casserole; cover and refrigerate up to 24 hours. Heat oven to 350°. Pour reserved milk mixture over potatoes. Bake uncovered 40 to 45 minutes or until hot. Stir potatoes before serving.

Slayton Chamber of Commerce

Winter's Day Seasoned Potatoes

3 medium potatoes, peeled and thinly sliced
1 medium onion, thinly sliced
1 teaspoon dried oregano, divided
1 teaspoon garlic powder, divided
2 tablespoons melted butter, divided
Salt and pepper, to taste

Place ½ potatoes and ½ onions in buttered 9x13-inch baking dish. Sprinkle with ½ oregano and ½ garlic powder and drizzle with 1 tablespoon butter. Repeat layers, ending with remaining butter. Season with salt and pepper. Cover and bake 20 minutes at 425°. Uncover and bake 15 additional minutes or until potatoes are tender.

Woodland Hill Winery

731 County Road 30 Southeast • Delano
763-972-4000 • www.woodlandhillwinery.com/winery

Nestled in a beautiful country setting, just west of Minneapolis, is Woodland Hill Winery. Visitors can relax and unwind while enjoying a glass of wine with friends and family. The tasting room offers a daily selection of featured wines, and each weekend there are tours of the vineyard and winery, giving visitors the opportunity to experience the wine making process. There is a quaint boutique onsite for that special gift, and, of course, all wines are available for purchase.

The Winery hosts a wide variety of events throughout the year... Fondue Fridays, Ladies Night Out, Lighted Hayride and Saturday Night Soup are just a few of these unique gatherings. Please visit their site for event details, list of wines and hours of operation.

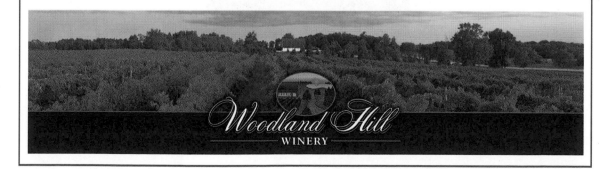

Honey-Mustard Glazed Carrots

½ cup water
1 bag baby carrots
2 tablespoons honey
1 tablespoon olive oil
2 teaspoons Dijon mustard
1 tablespoon chopped fresh parsley
¼ teaspoon salt
⅛ teaspoon pepper

In 2-quart saucepan, bring water to boil. Add carrots.
Cover; simmer 10 to 15 minutes or until tender. Drain.
In separate bowl, combine remaining ingredients. Add
carrots; toss lightly to coat.

Slayton Chamber of Commerce

Audubon Center of North Woods

Cheese-Scalloped Carrots

¼ cup butter
1 small onion, chopped
¼ cup flour
1 teaspoon salt
¼ teaspoon dry mustard
2 cups milk
⅛ teaspoon pepper
¼ teaspoon celery salt
2 to 3 pounds precooked sliced carrots
2 cups grated sharp Cheddar cheese
2 cups breadcrumbs
2 to 3 tablespoons butter, melted

Melt butter; add onion and cook 2 to 3 minutes. In separate bowl, combine flour, salt and mustard; add to butter mixture. Add milk and heat, stirring until smooth and slightly thickened. Add pepper and celery salt. In a 3-quart casserole arrange alternating layers of carrots, cheese and sauce ending with sauce. Mix breadcrumbs with melted butter. Arrange crumbs over top. Bake at 350° for 15 minutes, covered and 15 minutes uncovered.

Valerie (Aske) Olson and Carol Olson
Stand Still Parade

Calico Bean Bake

1 pound ground beef
1 cup chopped onion
½ pound bacon
½ cup ketchup
¾ cup brown sugar

2 teaspoons salt
1 teaspoon mustard
2 cans pork & beans, drained
2 cans butter beans, drained
2 cans kidney beans, drained

Brown ground beef, onion and bacon in skillet; drain. Add remaining ingredients and bake at 350° for 40 minutes.

Linda Yurcek
Younger Brothers Capture

Younger Brothers Capture

September

Madelia's Main Street
www.visitmadelia.com

On September 7, 1876, the James-Younger gang attempted to rob the First National Bank in Northfield and were driven off by the determined townsfolk, killing two members of the gang and wounding several more. Two citizens of Northfield also died as a result of the robbery and resulting gun battle. The surviving members of the gang escaped on horseback, not knowing

that the largest manhunt in the history of the United States was being formed to chase them down. For two weeks, the gang members eluded capture. On September 21, 1876, the travails of the Youngers and Pitts came to an end as they were captured by the Madelia's Magnificent Seven. The Younger Brothers Capture Celebration celebrates the capture of the Younger Brothers Gang outside of Madelia following the failed Northfield Bank Robbery. The festival centers on a re-enactment of the 1876 capture, with local actors portraying the historic roles.

Golden Beans Au Gratin

4 bacon slices
1 cup onion rings
½ pound Velveeta cheese, cubed
¼ cup milk
⅛ teaspoon salt
Dash of pepper
2 (9-ounce) bags frozen green beans, cooked and drained
1 cup seasoned croutons

Fry bacon until crisp; remove from skillet and set aside. Remove all but 1 tablespoon bacon grease from skillet. Cook onion in bacon grease until tender. Add cheese and milk; stir until melted. Crumble and stir in bacon, salt, pepper and beans. Pour into casserole dish, top with croutons and bake at 350° for 25 minutes.

Appeldoorn's Sunset Bay Resort

Escalloped Corn (Squaw Corn)

1 egg
1 can cream style corn
1 can whole kernel corn
1 cup soda cracker crumbs
2 teaspoons sugar
2 tablespoons flour
Salt and pepper
1 cup milk
2 tablespoons melted butter

Beat egg in casserole dish, add cream and whole kernel corns. In separate bowl, mix soda cracker crumbs, sugar, flour, salt and pepper; add to egg and corn mixture. Add milk and melted butter. Spread a few crackers crumbs on top and pour ¼ cup melted butter over all. Bake at 350° for 30 minutes.

Appeldoorn's Sunset Bay Resort

Tomato and Corn Scallop

1 jar Cheez Whiz
2 cans whole kernel corn,
   drained

1½ cups breadcrumbs, divided
4 tomatoes, sliced
⅓ cup butter, melted

Heat Cheese Whiz in saucepan over low heat. Add corn and
½ cup breadcrumbs. In casserole dish, layer ½ corn mixture
and top with ½ tomato slices. Repeat layers. Toss remaining
cracker crumbs in melted butter; sprinkle over casserole. Bake
at 350° for 30 minutes.

Joanne Toinette, Trenda's Cookbook
Taste of Shakopee

Taste of Shakopee

August

Huber Park
Shakopee, MN
www.tasteofshakopee.com

For almost 50 years, the Shakopee
Jaycees have been an active partner
in the community. From providing
individual opportunities to develop
personally and professionally, to
supporting multiple charities in
the area and around the world, the
Jaycees are the premier organization

for young people who wish to be active members in their community. The Shakopee Jaycees run over
a hundred events each year. From concessions at softball, to supporting youth events, to helping
provide for the homeless and for our soldiers overseas, the Shakopee Jaycees offer young people an
opportunity to enrich the world around them. Additionally, through many socials and celebrations,
members are encouraged to share their experiences, their passions, and their interests. In 2011, the
Shakopee Jaycees took over Taste of Shakopee. Taste of Shakopee is part of the kick-off of Derby
Days, a celebration in early August that includes games, vendors, a parade, and music. Taste of
Shakopee provides local restaurants with an opportunity to show off their best dishes and displays
for the community. Thousands of members of the Shakopee community come down to sample the
available foods and voice their opinion on the best dish and display.

Country Corn Casserole

3 tablespoons butter
3 ears fresh sweet corn, cut off cob
½ cup chopped green, yellow or red bell pepper
1 teaspoon dried basil leaves
½ teaspoon salt
1 medium ripe tomato cut into ½-inch cubes
1 tablespoon fresh chopped parsley

In 2-quart saucepan, melt butter. Stir in remaining ingredients except tomato and parsley. Cover; cook over medium heat, stirring occasionally, until vegetables are crisply tender (10 to 12 minutes). Remove from heat. Stir in tomato and parsley. Cover; let stand 1 minute or until tomato is heated through.

Sever's Corn Maze and Fall Festival

Sever's Corn Maze and Fall Festival

Open every Friday, Saturday and Sunday - mid September through end of October

**1100 Canterbury Road
Shakopee
952-974-5000
www.severscornmaze.com**

Sever's Corn Maze and Fall Festival has been welcoming thousands of visitors since 1997. It is located just west of Canterbury Park in Shakopee. It's a great way to spend the day and fun for all ages. Live music, great food, captivating magic and wildlife shows, pig races, and an awesome exotic animal petting zoo where guests can get up close and personal with kangaroos, camels  and more. Enjoy the huge straw bale maze that is perfect for all ages to climb and explore, jump into the massive corn pool with over 10,000 bushels of corn, bounce on the jumping pillows, we blast pumpkins and navigate the corn maze where everyone is eligible for prizes. Sever's has so many things to do and is so much fun. Great photo ops are located throughout the courtyard, and on the way out, find the perfect pumpkin in Sever's great pumpkin patch for this year's jack-o-lantern.

Corn Fritters

Vegetable oil
1¾ cups flour
2 teaspoons baking powder
1 teaspoon salt

¾ cup milk
1 egg
1 can whole corn

Pour enough oil in deep fryer to cover fritters, at least 2 cups; heat to 365°. In separate bowl, combine milk, egg and corn; stir well. Carefully drop ¼ cup mixture into hot oil. Fry until golden brown and drain on paper towels. Serve warm and enjoy.

Cara Sinn
Trimont Fun Fest

Corn Frittata

6 large eggs
⅓ cup 1% milk
2 tablespoons snipped fresh chives
½ teaspoon salt
¼ teaspoon black pepper
2 ears corn on the cob, husked and kernels removed
1 jar roasted red pepper, drained and sliced

Whisk eggs, milk, chives, salt and pepper in large bowl until well blended; stir in corn and red pepper. Spray medium nonstick skillet with nonstick spray and set over medium heat. Add egg mixture; cover and cook until eggs are set, 15 to 18 minutes (do not stir). Remove frittata from heat and let cool slightly, about 5 minutes. Cut frittata into 6 wedges and serve immediately.

Buttered Corn Days

Corn Bake

2 cups fresh corn kernels
1 (14.75-ounce) can cream corn
1 (8½-ounce) package corn muffin mix
1 cup low-fat buttermilk
2 tablespoons butter, melted

Preheat oven to 400°. Lightly grease 9x13-inch baking dish. Combine corn kernels, cream corn, corn muffin mix, buttermilk and butter. Pour into baking dish and bake 40 minutes or until golden and toothpick comes out clean.

Buttered Corn Days

Sleepy Eye

Rich in history, traditions and pride, Sleepy Eye welcomes visitors to experience all it has to offer. There is fishing and boating on Sleepy Eye Lake, beautiful parks, swimming at the Family Aquatic Center, a 3.12 mile Lake Trail, the Depot Museum, Linus Statue, St. Mary's Church and unique shops and retail businesses. There are terrific places to stay like the W.W. Smith Inn B & B, Inn of Seven Gables, Eagles Orchid Inn or camp on the shores of Sleepy Eye Lake. Year round there is great food, terrific celebrations and more.

Corn Casserole

½ cup margarine
1 (17-ounce) can whole-kernel corn, undrained
1 (14.75-ounce) can cream-style corn
1 (8.5-ounce) box corn muffin mix

2 eggs, slightly beaten
1 cup sour cream
Pinch of salt, pepper and sugar
1 cup shredded sharp Cheddar cheese

Preheat oven to 350°. Melt margarine in 9x13-inch baking dish. Add whole-kernel corn, cream-style corn and muffin mix; stir gently with fork. Add eggs; mix with fork. Drop sour cream by tablespoons in different areas on top of corn mixture; fold in gently. Add seasonings. Sprinkle with Cheddar cheese. Put in preheated oven and bake 20 to 30 minutes or until mixture is firm. Cool slightly before cutting into squares. Serves 12.

Buttered Corn Days

Broccoli Corn Casserole

½ cup butter
¼ teaspoon poultry seasoning
2 cups Pepperidge Farm herb
   stuffing mix
2 (12-ounce) bags frozen broccoli

2 cans cream style corn
½ small onion, finely diced
2 eggs
⅛ teaspoon pepper

In small pan, melt butter over medium heat. Stir in poultry seasoning until blended. Add stuffing mix; blend well and set aside. In large pan, cook broccoli until large pieces break apart, about 2 to 3 minutes. Drain well. Add cream style corn and onion to broccoli. Mix lightly. Add 1 egg at a time and mix well after each egg. Add 1½ cups buttered stuffing and pepper; mix well. Reserve ½ cup stuffing. Place broccoli mixture in an unbuttered 2-quart casserole dish. Sprinkle reserved stuffing over top. Bake uncovered at 350° approximately 1 hour.

Tip:

California blend vegetables may be substituted for broccoli. This makes a very colorful dish.

RibFest

RibFest

August

Riverfront Park
Vetter Stone Amphitheater
Downtown Mankato
507-389-3000

RibFest has become a staple for Southern Minnesota's summer festivities, especially with the recent re-location to the Riverfront Park located in downtown Mankato. Every year, Ribbers from all across the United States come to the Mankato and make some of the nation's tastiest ribs. However, many also enjoy coming for the entertainment, which features regional and national acts. All in all, Ribfest is a 4-day festival filled with friends, family, food, and great music...what else could you ask for?!

Broccoli Casserole

¼ onion, finely chopped
6 tablespoons butter, divided
2 tablespoons flour
½ cup water
1 (8-ounce) jar cheese spread
2 packages frozen broccoli, chopped, thawed and drained
3 eggs, well beaten
½ cup breadcrumbs

Sauté onion in 4 tablespoons butter, stir in flour and add water. Cook over low heat, stirring until mixture thickens and comes to a boil; blend in cheese. Combine sauce, broccoli and eggs; mix gently until blended. Pour into 1½-quart casserole. Bake at 350° for 30 to 45 minutes. Last 5 minutes, cover with bread-crumbs and dot with remaining butter. Bake till breadcrumbs are golden brown.

Culturfest

Stuffed Artichokes

3 large artichokes
1 cup vegetable oil
1 box Italian breadcrumbs
¼ cup parsley flakes
3 cloves garlic, chopped fine
Salt and pepper to taste
1 cup fresh grated Parmesan cheese

Wash artichokes thoroughly and clip all points with scissors; set aside. Combine remaining ingredients and mix well. Spread artichoke leaves until flexible and stuff between leaves with mixture. Add 1 inch water to deep skillet and place stuffed artichokes in water. Bring water to a boil, then reduce to simmer. Cover tightly with lid and cook 45 minutes or until leaves are tender. Watch carefully, adding more water if needed.

Baked Apples

4 apples, unpeeled and cut into 8 pieces
½ cup raisins
1 cup sugar
2 tablespoons flour
1 teaspoons cinnamon
1 cup heavy cream

Place apples and raisins in 2-quart baking dish. Mix together sugar, flour, cinnamon and cream. Pour mixture over apples. Bake at 350° for 1 hour or until apples are done.

Center Creek Orchard

Sweet Potato Apple Casserole

4 medium sweet potatoes
3 medium tart apples
2 tablespoons flour
2 tablespoons brown sugar

2 tablespoons butter
½ cup apple juice
½ pound bacon

Peel sweet potatoes and cut into ¼-inch slices. Peel, core and slice apples. Combine flour and sugar and lightly toss with sweet potatoes and apples. Grease casserole dish and alternately layer apples and sweet potatoes. Dot with butter. Add apple juice. Arrange bacon slices on top. Cover and bake at 350° for 35 minutes or until tender. Uncover and bake 5 to 10 minutes until bacon is crisp.

Pleasant Valley Orchard

Maple Glazed Sweet Potatoes with Bacon and Caramelized Onions

4 pounds sweet potatoes, peeled and cut in 1-inch chunks
2 tablespoons olive oil
½ teaspoon salt
½ teaspoon ground black pepper
6 slices smoked bacon
4 medium onions (1 pound), thinly sliced
¾ cup pure maple syrup
2 teaspoons fresh herbs of choice (optional)

Preheat oven to 425°. In a large bowl, combine sweet potatoes, olive oil, salt and black pepper; toss well. Spread sweet potato mixture onto a large rimmed baking sheet. Roast until browned and tender, about 40 minutes; stir after the first 20 minutes. In a large skillet, cook bacon over medium heat until crisp and brown, about 10 minutes; crumble into a bowl, reserving grease in skillet. Cook onions in bacon grease until browned, about 10 minutes, stirring frequently. Reduce heat to low and cook onions until very soft, brown, and sweet, another 10 to 15 minutes. Stir often. Add onions to bacon and set aside. Pour maple syrup into hot skillet and bring to rolling boil. Add herbs (optional) and boil syrup until reduced by half, 3 to 4 minutes. Place roasted sweet potatoes and onion-bacon mixture into skillet, stirring well. Serve warm.

Audubon Center of the North Woods

Bacon Wrapped Water Chestnuts

2 cans whole water chestnuts

1 pound package bacon, cut into thirds

Sauce:
½ cup white sugar

½ cup brown sugar

¾ cup ketchup

Dash Worcestershire sauce

Wrap chestnuts with bacon and secure with toothpick. Bake at 350° for 30 minutes or until brown. Drain grease. Combine sugars, ketchup and Worcestershire; whisk well. Pour sauce over chestnuts and bake 30 minutes. Makes about 45 chestnuts.

Joan Ruen
Bluffscape Amish Tours

Bluffscape Amish Tours

April through October:
Monday – Saturday 10am and 1:30pm

Located in the red Feed Mill
102 Beacon Street East • Lanesboro
507-467-3070 • www.bluffscape.com

Bluffscape Amish Tours of Lanesboro takes visitors on a fun, educational experience through the Amish countryside of Southeastern Minnesota. The 3 hour tour departs from Lanesboro and travels to an Amish farm home where guests can browse Amish-made quilts, shop at an Amish farmers market filled with fresh baked and canned goods, peruse Amish hand-made baskets, admire the craftsmanship of Amish wood furniture, munch on sweet, buttery cashew crunch, and purchase fruits and vegetables from Amish gardens while in season. The Bluffscape guides explain the Amish culture and the families that live there. For history buffs, the tour often makes a non-Amish stop at the oldest church in Fillmore County. This fantastic tour gives a peek inside one of the many cultures that make America truly special.

Italian Zucchini Pie

4 cups thinly sliced zucchini
1 cup chopped onion
¼ cup butter
¼ cup chopped parsley
¼ teaspoon basil
¼ teaspoon oregano leaves

2 eggs, beaten
2 cups shredded mozzarella
  cheese.
1 (8-ounce) package crescent rolls
2 tablespoons mustard

Add zucchini, onion and butter to skillet and cook over medium heat until tender, about 10 minutes. Add parsley, basil and oregano. In small bowl combine eggs and mozzarella cheese; mix well. Add to zucchini mixture. Separate crescent rolls into triangles. Press onto bottom and sides of ungreased deep glass pie pan. Spread mustard over crust. Pour zucchini mixture on top. Bake at 375° for 18 to 20 minutes or until center is set. Cover edges of crust with foil to prevent crust from getting too brown. Let stand 10 minutes before cutting.

Joan Johnson
Stand Still Parade

Wine baskets available on the Bluffscape Amish Tours

Mexican Goulash

1 pound bacon
1 box spaghetti pasta
1 can corn
1 can tomatoes
1 can lima beans, drained
1 can peas, drained

Prepare spaghetti according to directions on box. Fry the bacon and add it to the drippings. Then add corn, tomatoes, lima beans and peas. (Drain the liquid from the beans and peas). Season to taste.

Culturfest

Deardorff Orchards

Wild Rice & Toasted Almond Pilaf

2 cups wild rice
2 tablespoons olive oil
1 medium onion, finely diced
3 cups chicken broth
4 cups water
2 tablespoons butter
1 cup sliced almonds
Salt and pepper

Rinse rice in large sieve under cold water and drain well. Heat oil in 5-quart heavy pot over medium heat until hot. Add onion and sauté about 5 minutes. Add rice and cook, stirring, until fragrant, about 3 to 4 minutes. Stir in broth and water. Bring to boil. Reduce heat to low and simmer, covered, until rice is tender, about 1 hour. Let sit for 10 minutes, then drain.

While rice is cooking, melt butter in sauté pan until hot and foam subsides. Add almonds and brown 3 minutes. Add almonds to rice and season with salt and pepper to taste. Mix well.

Executive Chef Terry Dox
Ruttger's Bay Lake Lodge

Slow Cooker Stuffing

1 cup butter
2 cup chopped celery
1 cup chopped onion
1 teaspoon poultry seasoning
1½ teaspoon crumbled leaf sage
1½ teaspoons salt

½ teaspoon pepper
1 teaspoon leaf thyme, crumbled
2 eggs, beaten
4 cups chicken broth
12 cups dried breadcrumbs

Combine butter, celery, onion, poultry seasoning, sage, salt, pepper, thyme, eggs and broth together. Add crumbs; blend well. Place in slow cooker and cook 45 minutes on high. Reduce heat to low and cook 6 hours.

Margaret Chiglo
Stand Still Parade

Polar Pete Ice Tee Golf, Detroit Lakes Polar Fest

Spaghetti with Fresh Vegetables Sauce

2 tablespoons olive oil
1 medium onion, chopped
1 teaspoon dried basil
1 teaspoon dried oregano
1 garlic clove, minced
1 small zucchini, thinly sliced
4 ounces mushrooms, thinly sliced
1 green bell pepper, seeded, cored and diced
2 tomatoes, peeled and chopped
1 (6-ounce) can tomato paste
1 teaspoon sugar
1 (10-ounce) package spaghetti noodles
Parmesan cheese

Heat oil in heavy skillet over medium-high heat. Add onion, basil, oregano and garlic. Sauté until onion softens, about 5 minutes. Add zucchini, mushrooms and bell pepper. Reduce heat and cook 8 minutes. Add tomatoes, paste and sugar. Bring to boil while stirring constantly. Reduce heat and simmer 30 to 35 minutes. Meanwhile, cook spaghetti according to package directions. Top spaghetti pasta with sauce and garnish with freshly grated Parmesan cheese.

Judy Forst
Stand Still Parade

"Real" Mac & Cheese

16 ounces macaroni
16 slices American cheese
2 sticks butter, cut into tablespoons
2 eggs, beaten
4 cups 2% milk
1 cup shredded sharp Cheddar cheese
½ cup shredded mozzarella cheese
½ cup shredded Parmesan cheese
4 ounces cream cheese, cubed
Salt and pepper to taste

Cook macaroni till al dente; set aside. Place remaining ingredients in large pan. Cook over medium heat, stirring constantly. When butter and cheese has melted, add macaroni. Pour in 9x13-inch baking dish. Mixture will be very wet. Bake at 350° for 30 to 40 minutes until mixture is set. Do not cook too long or it will be dry. It should have just a little "jiggle" to it.

Topping (optional):
1 cup plain breadcrumbs
4 tablespoons melted butter
Salt and pepper to taste

Combine breadcrumbs, butter, salt and pepper with fork. Sprinkle on top for last 10 minutes of baking time.

Little Falls Convention and Visitors Bureau

Better-For-You Mac & Cheese

1¼ cup shredded sharp Cheddar cheese, divided
1¼ cup grated Parmesan cheese, divided
½ cup skim milk
2 eggs
½ cup light sour cream
2 to 3 tablespoons Dijon mustard
3 to 4 garlic cloves, minced
Fresh ground pepper and salt to taste
1 (16-ounce) bag frozen petite peas, thawed
1 head cauliflower, cut small and steamed
4 cups 100% whole wheat macaroni, cooked

Preheat oven to 350°. Spray casserole dish with nonstick cooking spray. In a large bowl, add 1 cup each cheeses, milk, eggs, sour cream, mustard, garlic, salt, pepper, peas and cauliflower. Mix ingredients together until combined. Prepare macaroni according to package directions. Add cooked macaroni and cheese mixture into warm pot macaroni was cooked in and stir. The residual heat will help mixture combine. Pour into prepared casserole dish. Sprinkle remaining Cheddar and Parmesan on top. Bake until the filling is hot and the topping is golden, about 35 to 40 minutes.

Culturfest

Easter Pizza

Crust:

Make standard double pie crust. Divide in half and roll out one into 9x13-inch baking dish. Set aside remaining crust.

Filling:

11 eggs, beaten
2 sticks pepperoni, sliced
1 pound shredded Colby Jack
    cheese

1 pound shredded American
    cheese
1 egg for topping

Combine 11 beaten eggs, pepperoni, and both cheeses; pour over crust in baking dish. Cover with second pie crust, crimp edges as you would a pie. Beat 1 egg and brush top of crust. Cut vent holes in top crust. Bake at 350° for 50 to 60 minutes. When a knife is inserted into center, no egg should be on knife.

Cindy Becker
Wadena Chamber of Commerce

Meat & Seafood

Chicken Stir-Fry

3 scallions, minced (divided)
4 tablespoons soy sauce (divided)
1 pound skinless, boneless chicken thighs, thinly sliced crosswise
1 teaspoon cornstarch
2 garlic cloves, minced
1 teaspoon minced, peeled fresh ginger
3 tablespoons plus 1 teaspoon peanut oil (divided)
2 eggs, beaten
3 cups cooked brown rice

Mix 2 scallions, 2 tablespoons soy sauce, chicken and cornstarch in a medium bowl. Marinade 10 minutes. In a non-stick skillet, stir-fry garlic and ginger in 2 tablespoons oil for 10 seconds. Add chicken and cook 4 minutes. Remove chicken and wipe out skillet. Cook eggs in 1 teaspoon oil in skillet, not stirring; when set, flip and cook for 30 seconds. Remove from skillet and dice. Stir-fry 1 scallion in 1 tablespoon oil for 15 seconds. Add rice; stir-fry for 7 minutes. Add chicken, eggs and 2 tablespoons soy sauce. Stir-fry 30 seconds, or until hot.

Bloomington Convention and Visitors Bureau

Marinated Chicken Wings

5 pounds wings (discard wing tips)
1 cup soy sauce
1 cup water
¼ cup oil
¼ cup sugar
¼ cup pineapple juice
¼ teaspoon salt
1 teaspoon ginger
1 teaspoon garlic powder

Wash wings and set aside. Combine remaining ingredients. Pour over wings and marinate 24 hours, no less. Bake at 350° for 45 to 60 minutes.

Shirley Uselman
Wadena Chamber of Commerce

Teriyaki Chicken Wings

1 cup water
1 cup soy sauce
1 cup sugar
¼ cup pineapple juice
¼ cup vegetable oil
1 teaspoon garlic powder
1 teaspoon ground ginger
5 pounds chicken wings

Mix all ingredients in a zip-lock bag and marinate overnight. Place on baking sheet and bake at 350° for 1 to 1½ hours; turn wings halfway through baking.

A maze'n Farmyard

County Fair Chicken Bake

¼ cup butter
½ cup diced celery, divided
½ cup chopped onion, divided
1 (6-ounce) package Stove Top Stuffing
    with Wild Rice
¼ cup toasted pecans
¼ cup dried cranberries

1⅔ cups hot water
1½ pounds cooked chicken, cubed into
    1-inch chunks
1 can cream of mushroom soup
⅓ cup sour cream
¼ cup white wine (optional)

In skillet over medium heat, melt butter and sauté ¼ cup celery and ¼ cup onion till tender. Mix stuffing, seasoning packet, pecans, cranberries, water and remaining celery and onions. Stir until stuffing is just moistened and other ingredients are mixed. Place chicken into 9x13-inch baking dish. Mix soup, sour cream and wine together and pour over chicken. Top with stuffing mixture and bake 30 minutes at 375°.

Douglas County Fair

Chicken Hotties

6 boneless chicken thighs
3 jalapeño peppers, seeded and cut each into 8 matchsticks
12 slices bacon, cut in half
Salt and pepper to taste
BBQ sauce

Cut thighs into 4 equal pieces, lay 1 jalapeño matchstick on each and wrap in bacon. Secure with toothpicks. Salt and pepper to taste. Grill over medium heat until bacon is crisp and chicken is cooked through, about 12 minutes. Brush with sauce and serve.

Shirley Uselman
Wadena Chamber of Commerce

Rosemary and Garlic Roasted Chicken

½ cup butter, softened
2 tablespoons crushed dried rosemary
2 tablespoons minced fresh parsley
3 garlic cloves, minced
1 teaspoon salt
½ teaspoon pepper
1 whole roasting chicken (5 to 6 pounds)

Mix butter and seasonings well; set aside. Wash chicken and pat dry. Place chicken, breast side up, on rack in roasting pan and tie drumsticks together with kitchen string. Spread butter mixture over chicken. Cover and bake at 350° for 1½ hours, basting every 30 minutes. Uncover; bake 30 to 50 minutes longer or until a thermometer reads 180°, basting occasionally. Cover loosely with foil and let rest 15 minutes before carving.

Slim's Woodshed

160 1st Street NW • Harmony
507-886-3114 • www.slimswoodshed.com

Slim's Woodshed and Museum is a fantastic stop for Minnesota Travelers. They have many types of wood, tools and supplies to meet all types of wood carving needs and interests. In the Wood Room,

they have the finest in Basswood, Butternut, and Catalpa, Box Specials for Basswood, Butternut, and Cottonwood Bark, Walking Sticks, Cypress Knees, Juniper Pine, Cutouts, and Roughouts. The Gift Shop offers the finest in Wood Carvings, Specialty Gifts, many different carving knives, gouges, and carving books. Guided tours are offered through the largest Woodcarving Museum in the United States which holds over 4000 carvings from all around the world! Be sure to also visit The Loft, featuring antiques and flea market items and the Classroom where carving classes are held weekly.

Chicken Hotdish

1 cup cooked chicken
1 cup cooked rice
1 can cream of mushroom soup
1 small onion
Salt to taste

½ cup Miracle Whip
1 teaspoon lemon juice
¾ cup chopped celery
2 hard boiled eggs
¼ cup slivered almonds

Preheat oven to 350°. Combine all ingredients and pour into casserole dish. Bake 30 minutes.

Northland Woolens

Slow Cooker Chicken in Mushroom Gravy

3 whole chicken breasts
Salt and pepper to taste
¼ cup cooking wine
1 can cream of mushroom soup

4 ounces mushrooms
1 cup sour cream
¼ cup flour

Place chicken in slow cooker. Season with salt and pepper. Combine wine and soup; pour over chicken. Add mushrooms. Cover and cook on low for 6 to 7 hours. Remove chicken. Stir sour cream and flour into gravy in slow cooker. Heat until warm. Serve chicken and gravy over rice, noodles, or potatoes.

Hyde-A-Way Bay Resort

Just a Jaunt

Tour, Taste and Shop your way through these unique establishments. With a mix of guided and self-tour experiences, each stop along the way provides interest to the individual and group traveler. Tailor your visit to include as many stops along the Jaunt as your time allows. The locations are truly "Just A Jaunt" from one site to the next. Contact each business for reservations or additional information.

Businesses included on the "Just A Jaunt" experience are Crooked Willow, Carlos Creek Winery, Tastefully Simple, Northland Woolens, Inc., Minnesota Lakes Maritime Museum, Lillians, Broadway Bistro and Just Like Grandma's. For detailed directions visit www.justajaunt.com.

Chicken Crêpes

Crêpes:

4 cups milk

12 eggs

2⅔ cups flour

In blender, combine milk, eggs and flour until smooth. Allow to rest at room temperature for 1 hour. Spray sauté with non-stick cooking spray and add enough crepe mixture to cover bottom. Cook until firm enough to turn over and finish cooking on opposite side. Entire cooking should take 2 to 3 minutes.

Filling:

10 tablespoons butter, divided

1 large onion, chopped

6 tablespoons flour

1⅓ cups chicken broth

1 cup half-and-half

1 teaspoon salt

½ teaspoon rosemary

½ pound mushrooms, sliced

1 pound fresh asparagus, chopped

4 cups chicken, cooked and diced

In saucepan, melt 4 tablespoons butter. Add onions and cook, stirring frequently. Add remaining butter and cook until melted. Add flour, stirring until bubbly. Gradually add broth and cream; cook, stirring until boils and thickens. Remove from heat. Add salt and rosemary. Add mushrooms, asparagus and chicken. Heat thoroughly, stirring frequently. Place mixture into individual crêpes and cover with Mornay Sauce.

Mornay Sauce:

½ cup butter

½ cup flour

4 teaspoons chicken bouillon

6 cups milk

2 cups Swiss cheese

1 cup Parmesan cheese

In saucepan, melt butter. Blend in flour and bouillon and cook until smooth and bubbly. Gradually add milk. Cook until mixture boils and thickens, stirring constantly. Add cheeses and stir until smooth.

Jail House Inn Bed & Breakfast
Preston Convention and Visitors Bureau

Chicken Tetrazzini

4 chicken breasts
6 cups chicken broth
1 pound sliced mushrooms
1 medium onion, chopped
½ cup butter
½ cup white wine
2 cans cream of chicken soup
1 (16-ounce) container sour
   cream

¾ pound (12 ounces) angel hair
   pasta, cooked
1 pound mozzarella cheese,
   shredded
½ cup fresh grated Parmesan
   cheese
1 teaspoon thyme

Boil chicken breasts in broth until done. Discard broth and cube chicken; set aside. Sauté mushrooms and onions in butter in skillet; set aside. In saucepan, combine wine, chicken soup and sour cream. Bring to a boil. Add chicken mixture to saucepan. In greased 9x13-inch pan, layer ½ cooked pasta, ½ chicken sauce, ½ mozzarella cheese. Repeat and top with Parmesan cheese. Bake at 300° for 30 to 40 minutes.

Albert Lea Convention and Visitors Bureau

Jailhouse Inn, Preston

Deluxe Hotdish

1 can cream of mushroom soup
1 can cream of chicken soup
1 can cream of celery soup
¼ cup French or Western dressing
1 box Uncle Ben's Long Grain and Wild Rice, prepared as
    directed on box
¼ cup butter, melted
4 cups cubed chicken, cooked
½ cup Parmesan cheese

Mix soups, Western dressing, prepared rice, and melted butter in a large bowl. Put ⅔ of the mixture into greased 9x13-inch pan. Cover with layer of chicken. Spread remaining ⅓ mixture on top of chicken. Cover with foil and bake at 350° for 1 to 1½ hours, until bubbly hot. Remove cover; sprinkle with Parmesan cheese. Return to oven 20 minutes or until brown.

A maze'n Farmyard

Chicken and Bacon Roll-Ups

½ cup reduced-fat mayonnaise
1 teaspoon minced fresh tarragon
2 teaspoons fresh lemon juice
4 (2.8-ounce) whole wheat flatbreads (such as Flatout)
2 cups shredded romaine lettuce
2 cups chopped tomato (about 2 medium)
4 center-cut bacon slices, cooked, drained and crumbled
2 cups shredded skinless, boneless rotisserie chicken breast

Combine reduced-fat mayonnaise, minced tarragon and fresh lemon juice in a small bowl. Spread 2 tablespoons mayonnaise mixture over each flatbread. Top each with ½ cup shredded romaine lettuce, ½ cup tomato, ¼ bacon and ½ cup chicken. Roll up.

Randy Mayor and Leigh Ann Ross
Little Falls Convention and Visitors Bureau

Cheesy Broccoli and Chicken Casserole

1½ cups shredded Cheddar cheese
½ cup chopped red bell pepper
½ cup light mayonnaise
1 can cream of celery sop
1 (8-ounce) can sliced water chestnuts, drained
1 (14-ounce) bag frozen broccoli florets, thawed (chop large pieces)
2 cups diced cooked chicken

Preheat oven to 375°. In large bowl, combine cheese, bell pepper, mayonnaise, soup and water chestnuts. Stir in broccoli and chicken; pour into greased baking dish. Bake 45 to 50 minutes or until hot and bubbly.

Slayton Chamber of Commerce

Axel's Spicy Penne

4 tablespoons olive oil
3 tablespoons chopped garlic
6 ounces white wine
1 (12-ounce) jar alfredo sauce
4 tablespoons basil pesto
2 pounds boneless, skinless chicken breast
4 teaspoons Cajun seasoning
2 pounds penne pasta, cooked
4 tablespoons sun-dried tomatoes
4 tablespoons Parmesan cheese

Heat oil in skillet over medium heat. Add garlic and sauté until aromatic. Deglaze with wine and cook until reduce by half. Add alfredo sauce and pesto; heat to 165°. Season chicken breast with Cajun spice and place in hot cast iron skillet. Cook to 165°; remove and cut into ½-inch strips. Add pasta to skillet pan with heated sauce; toss to evenly coat. Place pasta into pasta bowl and top with chicken. Garnish with sun-dried tomatoes and Parmesan cheese.

Roseville Convention and Visitors Bureau

Cove Point's Lucca Pasta

Sauce:

1 cup heavy whipping cream
1 cup 2% milk
2 tablespoons chicken bouillon
2 tablespoons Cajun seasoning

2 tablespoons paprika
1 teaspoon cayenne
4 ounces melted butter
½ cup flour

Combine cream, milk, chicken bouillon and seasonings in saucepan. Heat cream mixture to simmer and reduce heat to low. In separate pan, melt butter and add flour slowly, creating a roux. Add roux mixture to cream and stir until roux is cooked through and sauce has thickened. Set aside.

Pasta:

1 medium chicken breast, cubed
2 tablespoons butter
½ red bell pepper, julienne

½ green bell pepper, julienne
½ red onion, julienne
3 cups cooked penne pasta

Sauté cubed chicken breast in butter with julienned peppers and onion. When cooked through, add penne pasta and prepared sauce. Toss well and serve. Serves 2.

Cove Point Lodge

Grilled Bacon-Wrapped Waterfowl

4 pounds goose or duck meat
3 pounds thinly sliced bacon
Garlic salt

Cut waterfowl into pieces approximately ¾ to 1-inch thick. Cut bacon strips in half. Wrap duck or goose pieces with halved bacon strip and secure with toothpick. Place on platter for grilling and sprinkle with garlic salt. Heat grill to medium. Grill bacon-wrapped fowl slowly until bacon and meat is browned and cooked through. Turn often to ensure even cooking.

Detroit Lake Polar Fest

Pheasant Meatloaf

2 slices bread
12 ounces whipping cream
1 pound ground turkey
Salt and pepper
1 clove garlic
2 eggs

1.8 ounces fried mushrooms
3.6 ounces pecans
2 sprigs thyme
2 pheasant breasts
Bacon slices

Trim away crusts on bread slices and dice. Soak in cream 10 minutes. Mix ground turkey with salt, pepper, garlic, egg and cream-soaked bread. Chop mushrooms and nuts coarsely and mix them well with thyme. Add to ground turkey mixture. Slice pheasant breasts lengthwise into 3 strips each. Grease loaf baking pans and line with bacon. Fill pans alternately with ground turkey mixture and pheasant slices, ending with ground turkey. Fold bacon strips on top. Bake at 350° for 45 to 50 minutes.

Wayne Jenum
Glenwood Chamber of Commerce

City of Glenwood

320-634-3636
7 Frist Street NW, Glenwood
www.GlenwoodLakesArea.org
Find us on Facebook

www.GlenwoodLakesArea.org

Glenwood sits on the eastern shores of Lake Minnewaska in central Minnesota. Glenwood is widely known for its beauty and the view of the lake coming down the hill in to town. There are many historic places to visit, parks and trails. Each year there are several festivals and celebrations for locals and visitors alike. The Glenwood Lakes Area Chamber of Commerce works to promote the area through a variety of ways, including plenty of free family events, all year long. Visit their website to learn more and to see a full calendar of area events.

Winterama
Food, Fun, and Fireworks
Early February

**The Main Event
– International
Hetteen Vintage
Snowmobile Races**
Early March

**Pope County
Community Expo**
Late March or early April

Kids Day
1st Saturday in June

Waterama
Great Summertime Fun for the entire family
End of July

Pope County Free Fair
August

Pope County Fright Nights
October
Dare to be Scared?!

Magical Christmas in Glenwood
Free Old, Fashioned Family Fun Thursday nights between Thanksgiving and Christmas

Jumbo Shells

1 box jumbo pasta shells
½ cup chopped onion
1 garlic clove, minced
2 tablespoons oil
1 teaspoon salt
2 tablespoons chili sauce
1 (6-ounce) can tomato paste
3 cups tomato juice
½ teaspoon sugar

¼ teaspoon pepper
1 pound ricotta cheese
1 pound cottage cheese
½ pound mozzarella cheese
2 eggs, beaten
1 teaspoon parsley
1 pound ground beef
1 medium onion, chopped

Cook shells according to package directions; set aside. Sauté onion and garlic in oil. Add salt, chili sauce, tomato paste, tomato juice, sugar and pepper. Simmer 10 minutes; set aside. In large bowl, combine ricotta cheese, cottage cheese, mozzarella cheese, the beaten eggs and parsley. Mix together. Brown hamburger and onion together, drain and put into cheese mixture. In casserole dish, pour in ½ of tomato mixture. Stuff each cooked shell with meat and cheese filling. Arrange in casserole dish. Pour remaining tomato mixture on top. Bake at 350° for 30 minutes.

Joanne Toinette, Trenda's Cookbook
Taste of Shakopee

Meatloaf

2 pounds ground beef
1 pound ground pork
1 teaspoon salt
½ cup milk
2 cups Rice Krispies

½ teaspoon pepper
⅓ cup ketchup
2 eggs, slightly beaten
1 teaspoon Worcestershire
   sauce

Preheat oven to 375°. Combine all ingredients, mixing well.
Shape in loaf pan.

Sauce:

3 tablespoons brown sugar
¼ teaspoon nutmeg

¼ cup ketchup
1 teaspoon dry mustard

Whisk together all ingredients and spoon on top of meatloaf.
Bake 45 minutes.

Culturfest

Granny's Applesauce Meatloaf

1 pound ground beef
¾ cup applesauce
½ cup breadcrumbs

½ cup diced onion
2 eggs, beaten
½ teaspoon salt

Preheat oven to 350°. Mix ground beef, applesauce, breadcrumbs,
onion, eggs and salt. Spoon into an ungreased 9x5-inch loaf pan;
set aside.

Topping:

¼ cup ketchup
2 tablespoons mustard

¼ cup packed brown sugar

Combine ketchup, mustard and brown sugar; spread over meatloaf.
Bake 1 hour. Serves 6 to 8. Serve with mashed potatoes and fresh
green beans.

Slayton Chamber of Commerce

Swedish Meatballs with Gravy

4 pounds ground beef
2 pounds lean pork
2 cups dry breadcrumbs
¼ cup chopped onion
3 eggs, beaten
2 cups cold milk
½ teaspoon allspice

1 teaspoon pepper
3 teaspoons salt
1½ cups flour, divided
½ cup shortening
1 cup chicken stock, divided
2 cups water

Combine beef, pork, breadcrumbs, onion, eggs and milk. Shape into 1½-inch balls. Combine allspice, pepper, salt and 1 cup flour. Roll meatballs in flour. Brown balls on all sides in shortening in Dutch oven. Mix ½ cup flour, 1 cup chicken stock and water. Pour over meatballs. Reduce heat and simmer 50 minutes. If gravy is too thin, thicken with small amount of flour and water. Makes 40 meatballs.

Culturfest

Delicious Barbecued Meatballs

Meatballs:
6 cups ground beef
1 cup milk
2 cups quick oats
2 eggs
1 cup chopped onions (optional)

2 teaspoons salt
½ teaspoon pepper
¾ teaspoon chili powder
½ teaspoon garlic powder

Combine all meatball ingredients. Form into balls and place in 9x13-inch baking dish.

Sauce:
2 cups ketchup
½ cup chopped onions (optional)
1 cup brown sugar

¼ teaspoon chili powder
2 teaspoons liquid smoke

Mix sauce ingredients and pour over meatballs. Bake at 350° for 1 hour.

R&M Amish Tours

Sweet-N-Sour Meatballs

1 pound ground beef
1 cup soft breadcrumbs
1 egg, slightly beaten
2 tablespoons minced onion
2 tablespoons milk
½ teaspoon salt
⅛ teaspoon pepper
1 tablespoon vegetable oil
⅔ cup chili sauce
⅔ cup grape or red jelly

Combine ground beef, breadcrumbs, egg, onion, milk, salt, pepper and oil. Mix well and form into 40 bite-size meatballs, about the size of a teaspoon. Add oil to skillet and brown meatballs lightly over medium heat. Reduce heat, cover and cook over low heat 5 minutes. Drain off excess fat. Combine chili sauce and jelly, pour over meatballs. Continue cooking, stirring occasionally, until jelly is melted. Simmer 10 to 12 minutes until sauce is thickened, basting occasionally.

Appeldoorn's Sunset Bay Resort

Beef Burrito Skillet

1 pound ground beef
1 package taco seasoning
1 can kidney beans, rinsed
1 cup salsa

1 cup water
4 flour tortillas, cut into 1½-inch
  strips
1 cup shredded Cheddar cheese

Brown ground beef; drain. Add taco seasoning, beans, salsa and water. Bring to boil, reduce heat and simmer 5 minutes. Add tortilla strips. Top with cheese, cover and let stand until cheese melts.

Hyde-A-Way Bay Resort

Texas Hash

2 cups sliced onion
¾ cup chopped green bell pepper
3 tablespoons shortening
1 pound ground beef
1 can stewed tomatoes
1 teaspoon salt
½ cup uncooked rice
½ teaspoon chili powder

Cook onion and green bell pepper in shortening until onion is soft and yellow. Add meat and brown; drain. Add remaining ingredients. Pour in greased casserole. Bake 1 hour at 350°.

Culturfest

Beef Stroganoff

¼ cup butter	1 tablespoon prepared mustard
2 medium onions, sliced thin	2 tablespoons brown sugar
2½ pounds round steak	Dash Worcestershire sauce
1 can tomato soup	½ pint sour cream
1 (1-ounce) can mushrooms	Salt and pepper

Melt butter in skillet over medium heat. Sauté onions until slightly browned. Remove onions and set aside. Brown steak, cubed or cut in thin strips, in same pan. Add remaining ingredients and cook slowly for 1 hour. Serve on top of rice or pasta.

Northern Rail Traincar Inn

1730 Highway 3 • Two Harbors
877-834-0955 • 218-834-0955 • www.northernrail.net

Northern Rail Traincar Inn offers a completely unique North Shore experience! Each room is created from authentic traincars renovated into gracious bed and bath suites. Northern Rail is set on 160 forested acres north of Two Harbors, near the intersection of Highway 61 and Highway 3. Just 23 minutes from Duluth, guests enjoy quick, convenient access to all the North Shore's amazing activities including the Superior Hiking Trail, State Snowmobile Trail system, and Gooseberry Falls. Northern Rail features 17 elegant Northwoods, Victorian, Oriental and Safari themed guestrooms housed in actual train boxcars and connected by a charming enclosed platform. The depot-style main building includes check-in, lending library and the continental breakfast area. Come enjoy the natural beauty of the North Shore of Lake Superior at Northern Rail Traincar Inn!

Tavern Burgers

1½ pounds ground beef
1 small onion, chopped
1 can tomato soup
1 tablespoon mustard
1 tablespoon vinegar

2 tablespoons brown sugar
2 tablespoons ketchup
Dash of Worcestershire sauce
Salt and pepper to taste

Brown ground beef and onion; drain. Place ground beef and remaining ingredients in slow cooker. Simmer on low 2 to 3 hours. The longer it simmers, the better it tastes! Serve on hamburger buns.

Joan Ruen
Bluffscape Amish Tours

Sloppy Joes

¼ cup mustard
¾ cup water
¼ cup vinegar
¼ cup sugar

1¾ cups ketchup
2 pounds ground beef
1 onion, chopped

In saucepan, combine mustard, water, vinegar, sugar and ketchup. Simmer 15 minutes. Do not skip this step; the simmering is important! Brown beef and onion; drain. Add sauce to ground beef. Place on buns and enjoy!

Joan Johnson
Stand Still Parade

Pat's Crumble Burgers

This is a delicious, quick and easy warm sandwich.

5 pounds ground beef
1 can cream of celery soup
2 cans ream of onion soup
Salt and pepper to taste

Brown and drain ground beef. Add soups, salt and pepper. Simmer 20 minutes. Serve on buns.

Pat Mulso
Freeborn County Historical Museum

Freeborn County Historical Museum, Library and Village

1031 Bridge Avenue • Albert Lea
507-373-8003 • www.fchm.us

Admission: Adults $5.00,
Students 12 to 18 - $1.00

Members and children 11 and
under Free

Household Memberships
begin at just $25.00 annually

Take I-90 Exit 157 and turn south to this complex located at the south edge of the Fairgrounds. The museum is a two level, air conditioned building, currently about 12,000 square feet with an additional 10,000 square feet under construction with completion scheduled for late 2013. Displays include a kitchen and living room of yesteryears, musical instruments, toys, dolls, medical exhibits and local history. The historical village includes the first log cabin in Freeborn County, a one room school house, General Store, Blacksmith Shop, Woodworking Shop, Post Office, Village Church, Hardware Store, working mill, shoe shop, barbershop, jail, bank, train depot, photo studio and a 170 foot long red exhibit building with numerous displays.

Stuffed Peppers

½ tablespoon minced garlic
1 cup diced tomatoes
½ pound finely minced onions
½ pound mushrooms, shredded
½ pound carrots, shredded
2½ cups tomato sauce
Basil, parsley, dill, salt and pepper to taste
1½ cups brown rice, cooked and cooled
1¼ pound feta cheese, crumbled
1 pound ground beef
12 green bell peppers, tops and seeds removed
Olive oil to drizzle on top of peppers
½ pound Cheddar cheese, shredded

Sauté garlic and veggies in butter or oil until tender, add tomato sauce and spices. Add rice; cool. Add feta cheese. Brown beef and drain; add to rice/veggie/cheese mixture. Taste for seasoning. Drizzle oil over peppers. Stuff with filling mixture. Bake 50 minutes at 325°; add shredded Cheddar cheese over top and continue to bake another 10 to 15 minutes, until melted.

Audubon Center of the North Woods

Italian Stuffed Peppers

4 green bell peppers
⅔ cup cooked rice
¼ cup olive oil, plus additional tablespoon
1 pound ground beef
2 tablespoons minced onion
1 tablespoon minced parsley
1 teaspoon salt, divided
¾ teaspoon pepper, divided
1½ cups canned tomatoes, drained
¼ cup water
¼ cup minced celery
Mozzarella cheese

Cut top from each pepper. Remove white fiber and seeds; rinse cavities. Drop into boiling salted water to cover and simmer 5 minutes. Remove peppers from water; invert and set aside to drain. Cook rice. Heat ¼ cup olive oil in skillet and add ground beef; brown and drain. Stir in onion, parsley, ½ teaspoon salt and ¼ teaspoon pepper. Mix with cooked rice. Lightly fill peppers with rice and meat mixture, heaping slightly. Place into baking dish. Pour around peppers a mixture of tomatoes, water, celery, 1 tablespoon olive oil, ½ teaspoon salt and ¼ teaspoon pepper. Place a strip of mozzarella cheese on top of each pepper. Bake at 350° for 15 minutes.

Culturfest

Polish Hotdish

2 pounds lean ground beef
1½ to 2 cups chopped celery
1 large onion, chopped
1 (28-ounce) jar Ragu chunky garden style roasted red peppers and onion sauce

1 (28-ounce) jar Ragu chunky garden style super mushroom sauce
1 or 2 (8-ounce) cans mushrooms with liquid
1½ (12-ounce) packages Kluski egg noodles

Preheat oven to 350°. Brown ground beef, celery and onions. If ground beef is not lean, add water and drain to degrease it. Add Ragu sauces and mushrooms. Cook Kluski noodles according to package directions. Drain and stir into meat mixture. Pour into large casserole or roaster and bake at 350° for 1 hour.

Sr. JoAnne Backes, OSB, St. Benedict's Monastery, St. Joseph
Stearns History Museum

Hamburger Pie

1 pound ground beef
½ cup chopped onion
½ teaspoon salt
Dash black pepper
1 can green beans, drained

1 can tomato soup
5 medium potatoes, cooked and
  mashed
1 egg, beaten
½ cup shredded cheese

In a large skillet, cook beef and onion until beef is lightly browned and onion is tender; drain. Add salt and pepper. Stir in green beans and soup. Pour into greased 1½-quart casserole. Prepare mashed potatoes, adding milk, butter and seasoning as you usually would and stir in egg. Spread potato mixture over meat and vegetables in casserole. Sprinkle cheese over potatoes. Bake at 350° for 25 to 30 minutes.

Elaine Olson
Stand Still Parade

Hungarian Goulash

1 pound beef stew meat
1 clove garlic, minced
2 medium onions, sliced
2 teaspoons paprika
1 teaspoon salt

½ teaspoon pepper
2 bouillon cubes
2 cups boiling water
1 cup hot water
2 cups diced potatoes

Cut meat into 1-inch cubes and brown in skillet, adding a bit of oil if needed. Add garlic, onions, paprika, salt and pepper. Dissolve bouillon cubes in boiling water and add to mixture. Cover and simmer 2½ hours. Add hot water and potatoes. Cook 20 minutes longer or until potatoes are tender.

Culturfest

Cabbage Rolls (Golabki)

This recipe is a festival tradition, year after year.

1 head cabbage
½ cup rice
1 onion, chopped fine
2 tablespoons butter
1 pound ground beef

½ pound ground pork or veal
1 egg
Salt and pepper to taste
5 slices bacon

Remove and dispose of cabbage core. Scald cabbage in boiling water, removing a few leaves at a time to avoid wilting. Set aside and cool completely. Stir rice into 2 quarts rapidly boiling water and boil 10 minutes; strain. Run cold water through rice in strainer. The rice will be half-cooked. Sauté onion in butter until transparent, watching carefully so it does not yellow. Combine rice, onion, meat, egg, salt and pepper; mix well. Lay out cabbage leaves and spread each with rice mixture, about ½-inch thick. Fold two opposite sides and roll, starting with one of the open ends. Fasten with toothpick. Place cabbage rolls in baking dish, cover with bacon and cook uncovered 2 hours at 300°. Baste occasionally. If using frying pan, add 1 cup water or tomato puree and simmer slowly 2 hours. Delicious served with mushroom sauce, tomato sauce or sour cream. When reheated the next day, they are even more delicious.

Courtesy of Polanie Club, Minneapolis
Treasured Polish Recipes for Americans Cookbook
Twin Cities Polish Festival

While in town for the Twin Cities Polish Festival...

Visit the Polish Library at the Polish American Cultural Institute of Minnesota (PACIM). The library is a treasure trove of contemporary and classic Polish language titles with over 5,000 books, audio books, film and music CDs and DVDs for adults and children. PACIM showcases Polish culture, history, people, and arts through its programs and events. www.pacim.org

PACIM

POLISH AMERICAN
CULTURAL INSTITUTE OF MINNESOTA

Easy Chow Mein

1 pound hamburger
2 cups chopped celery
1 can chicken with rice soup
1 can cream of chicken soup

1 can vegetable beef soup
1 can chicken with rice soup
1 can cream of chicken soup
1 can vegetable beef soup

Brown ground beef celery; drain fat. In casserole dish, combine hamburger mixture and soups; mix well. Bake 45 minutes at 350°. Serve with chow mein noodles.

Kathy Plank
Stockyard Days

Chinese Noodle Casserole

1 onion, chopped
Butter
1½ pounds ground sausage
1 green bell pepper, chopped
4 cups water

1¼ cups uncooked rice
1 small bunch celery, chopped
2 packages noodle soup mix
1 cup slivered almonds

Sauté chopped onion in small amount of butter; add sausage and cook thoroughly. Drain grease and add remaining ingredients. Pour into greased casserole. Bake covered at 325° for 1 hour.

Culturfest

Minotte's Steak Sinatra

This family classic was handed down by my father, Nick, who served this dish to 'old Blue Eyes' himself at his restaurant in Minneapolis back in 1971. Frank was quoted as saying "Big Nick, this is the best d*!@ steak I've ever had."

2 (12-ounce) USDA Choice or higher New York Strips
3 tablespoons olive oil
3 cloves garlic, fresh chopped
4 ounces yellow onions, julienned
4 ounces green peppers, julienned
8 ounces fresh portabella mushrooms, sliced
3 ounces roasted red peppers (canned)
¾ cup spaghetti sauce
Salt and pepper to taste
4 ounces Provolone, shredded mozzarella or gorgonzola
   crumbles (your choice)

Preheat grill. While grill is heating, add oil to large skillet and sauté garlic 1 minute, add onion, peppers and portabellas. Cook al dente and add roasted red peppers, mixing well. Turn off heat. Salt and pepper steaks and put on grill. Cook to personal preference; remove and let rest. Transfer steaks to oven-safe platter. Divide vegetable mixture evenly and place on top of steaks. Preheat oven on broil. Divide spaghetti sauce, and drizzle over each steak. Divide cheese of your choice; top each steak. Broil 2 to 3 minutes until cheese is melted.

Alexander Minotte, Executive Chef
Spirit Lake Steakhouse

French Dip

3 to 4 pound rump or chuck
   roast
1 can beef broth
1 can water

½ packet dry Italian dressing
1 packet dry au jus
Buns

Place all ingredients in slow cooker and cook 3 to 4 hours on high. Remove and slice thinly. Return to juice. Serve on buns with juice for dipping.

Hyde-A-Way Bay Resort

Beef and Pork Roast

2 pounds boneless chuck roast
2 pounds boneless pork roast
1 onion, sliced
2 cloves garlic, minced
2 bay leaves

1 teaspoon salt
½ teaspoon freshly ground
  pepper
6 potatoes
6 large carrots

Preheat oven to 400°. Arrange roasts in heavy Dutch oven.
Place in oven 10 minutes to brown meat on one side. Flip meat,
return to oven for additional 10 minutes. Arrange onion, garlic,
and bay leaf in pan and sprinkle with salt and pepper. Place
potatoes and carrots on top and cover. Reduce heat to 300° and
cook 1½ hours. Remove roast and place on platter. Let rest 10
to 15 minutes. Slice and serve.

Wabasha Street Caves

Nickelodeon Resort, Bloomington

Pork Medallions with Mango

2 tablespoons butter
2 pounds pork tenderloin medallions
¾ cup finely chopped red onion
1 clove garlic, minced
1 teaspoon curry powder
¼ cup flour
1 cup pork or chicken broth
1 large ripe mango, cut into chunks
½ cup heavy cream
½ teaspoon cinnamon

Heat butter in skillet. Brown medallions 2 to 3 minutes on each side and remove from pan. Add onion and garlic to skillet and cook until soft. Add curry powder and flour and stir until bubbly. Gradually stir in broth. Return medallions to broth mixture and cook over low heat about 10 minutes. Add mango to skillet and cook until heated through. Transfer medallions and mango to serving platter. Return sauce to high heat and add cream and cinnamon. Pour sauce over medallions.

Sous Chef Todd Diemert
Ruttger's Bay Lake Lodge

Pork Chops and Apples

6 pork chops
2 tablespoons butter
4 apples, peeled, cored and sliced
¼ cup brown sugar
½ teaspoon cinnamon

Brown pork chops on both sides in butter. Place apple slices in greased baking dish. Combine brown sugar and cinnamon and sprinkle over apples. Add pork chops. Cover and bake at 325° for 1½ hours.

Pleasant Valley Orchard

Pleasant Valley Orchard

17325 Pleasant Valley Road • Shafer
651-257-9159 • www.pleasantvalleyorchard.com

Pleasant Valley Orchard is located near Taylors Falls overlooking the scenic St. Croix Valley. Pleasant Valley Orchard's pick-your-own strawberry season is in June/July. The fall orchard season, featuring favorite Minnesota Grown apples, begins Labor Day weekend and runs through mid-November.

Pleasant Valley Orchard offers a fun fall experience for the whole family. Situated as it is, the orchard offers sweeping views of the St. Croix Valley in full fall dress. Guests enjoy the charm of the apple shed and vintage barn. In addition to favorite Minnesota Grown apples, there are an amazing array of pumpkins, a bakery and gift shop. The Orchard offers traditional orchard activities including pick-your-own weekends, hayrides, farm animals, kid's corral, nature trail and picnic area.

Bob Lauer's Father's Rib Recipe

Rib Rub:

¼ cup cane sugar
¼ cup brown cane sugar
¼ cup smoked paprika
3 tablespoons coarse sea salt
1 tablespoon fresh ground black
   pepper

1 tablespoon garlic powder
1 tablespoon onion salt
1 tablespoon chili powder
½ tablespoon cayenne pepper

Combine all ingredients and mix well. Set aside.

Ribs:

1 cup mayonnaise
1½ cups ketchup
3 tablespoons Tabasco sauce

1 or 2 racks St. Louis pork spare ribs
2 to 3 tablespoons Rib Rub
1 teaspoon onion powder

Preheat oven to 350°. Combine mayonnaise, ketchup and Tabasco sauce; whisk until well blended. Place in refrigerator. Trim excess fat from ribs and remove membrane from back. Rub all over with rub and onion powder. Wrap in heavy duty foil. Let rest at room temperature 30 minutes and place bone side down on baking sheet. Bake 1½ hours. Remove from oven, carefully unwrap and cool 15 minutes on wire rack. Brush both sides of ribs with prepared sauce and broil bone side up about 4 inches from coils. After 7 minutes turn ribs bone side down and brush with additional sauce. Broil additional 5 to 7 minutes and turn off oven and let ribs stay in closed oven 15 minutes. Do not try to make these on a grill because the sauce will burn!

Big Island Rendezvous

Country-Style Pork Ribs

3 pounds country-style pork loin ribs
2 cups ketchup
½ cup cider vinegar
⅓ cup packed dark brown sugar
3 tablespoons spicy brown mustard
3 tablespoons Worcestershire sauce
1 tablespoon liquid smoke
1 tablespoon chili powder
1 teaspoon salt
1 teaspoon coarse ground black pepper

Place ribs in greased slow cooker. Combine remaining ingredients and pour over ribs. Cover; cook on low heat setting 9 to 10 hours. Makes 6 servings.

Slayton Chamber of Commerce

Kerin Fahland

1 pound ground venison
¼ cup chopped yellow onion
¼ cup chopped celery
¼ cup chopped green bell pepper
2 cans diced tomatoes
1 can pork and beans
1 can pinto beans
1 can kidney beans
2 tablespoons chili spice
1 tablespoon garlic powder
1 cayenne pepper
1 (6-ounce) can tomato sauce
4 cups water
1 teaspoon salt
1 teaspoon pepper
¼ cup corn masa for thickener

Brown venison with chopped onions, celery and bell pepper. Add remaining ingredients and simmer 1 hour. Garnish with sour cream, shredded Cheddar cheese and chopped onion. Delicious served with cornbread.

Agate Days Celebration

Venison Stroganoff

2 pounds boneless venison loin or steak
¼ cup butter
6 ounces sliced mushrooms
21 ounces condensed beef broth, divided
⅓ cup minced onions
¼ cup tomato paste
1½ teaspoons garlic salt
⅓ cup flour
2 cups sour cream

Cut meat into strips. Melt butter in large skillet. Cook and stir mushrooms in butter 5 minutes; remove mushrooms. Using the same skillet, brown meat. Reserve ⅔ cup broth; set aside. Stir in remaining broth, onion, tomato paste and garlic salt. Cover and simmer 15 minutes. Blend reserved broth and flour; stir into meat. Add mushrooms, heat to boiling, stirring constantly. Boil and stir 1 minute. Stir in sour cream. Top with traditional Russian topping of potato straws.

Visit Brainerd

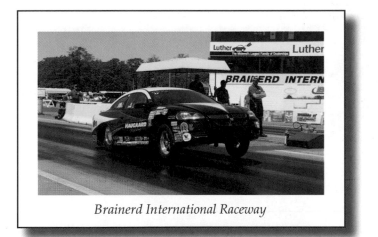

Brainerd International Raceway

Tasty Tilapia

6 tilapia fillets
1 cup brown sugar
1 teaspoon cumin

1 teaspoon cayenne
1 dash seasoning salt
1 dash garlic powder

Rinse fillets and pat semi-dry; set aside. Combine remaining ingredients in bowl. Rub mixture onto fillets. Place in greased pan and bake at 375° for 15 minutes.

Dick Dahlen
Big Island Rendezvous

Big Island Rendezvous and Festival

First Full Weekend in October

Albert Lea
800-658-2526

Declared one of the "Top 100 Festivals in North America" by the American Bus Association in Washington, DC, Big Island Rendezvous hosts 1,000 re-enactors who create a 45-acre community celebrating everything from 1670 to 1880 in early America. There is a woodland Indian camp and a pioneer town complete with chuck wagon, stagecoach and hearses from the 1880's. President and Mary Todd Lincoln are present to witness live round cannon fire, and Benjamin Franklin also attends to spark a conversation with visitors as they walk through 250 campsites. Blacksmiths, woodworkers, candle makers, silversmiths and potters sell their wares. Music by regional bluegrass, Irish or Celtic musicians fill the air, and Scottish dancers and cloggers perform each day. Smoked bbq ribs, gyros, pulled pork sandwiches, pork chops on a stick, buffalo burgers, kettle corn, Indian tacos and funnel cakes are available as visitors experience "life in another century".

Tantalizing Tilapia

1 box Zatarain's Jambalaya rice mix
1 (6-ounce) can pineapple juice, divided
2 tilapia fillets
8 cinnamon graham crackers, finely crushed
1 (10-ounce) can diced tomatoes with green chilies, divided
6 medium size frozen cooked shrimp, thawed, cut into ¼-inch bits
4 green olives, chopped (optional)
1 bunch baby spinach, washed and stems removed
1 lemon, sliced

Prepare Jambalaya rice according to package directions. Reserve ⅓ pineapple juice; set aside. Rinse fillets and submerge in remaining ⅔ pineapple juice. Place fillets in zip-lock bag with crushed graham crackers and coat both sides. Combine ½ diced tomatoes, shrimp and olives; set aside. When rice is nearly done, oil fry pan and cook fillets on medium heat; add a little butter to help browning. Flip fillets when brown on bottom. Toss spinach in saucepan with 1-inch water and cook until leaves are wilted. Add remaining ⅓ pineapple juice and ½ diced tomatoes to rice. Make bed of spinach on plate for fillets. Place fillets on spinach beds and cover with tomato mixture. Add rice to side and garnish with lemon slices.

Brian Vickery
Stockyard Days

Potato-Crusted Walleye with Cucumber Sour Cream Dressing

Cucumber Sour Cream Dressing:

4 ounces cream cheese, softened

1 cup sour cream

4 ounces cucumbers, halved lengthwise, seeded and cut into 2-inch pieces

1 teaspoon dry dill weed

½ teaspoon kosher salt

1 tablespoon Dijon mustard

⅛ teaspoon white pepper

1 teaspoon fresh lemon juice

1 ounce green onions, cut into ⅛-inch pieces

Place cream cheese and sour cream in blender and process until smooth. Add remaining ingredients and process until cucumbers are pureed. Set aside.

Potato Crust:

2 tablespoons butter

3 tablespoons dry dill weed

3 tablespoons paprika

2 teaspoons white pepper

2 cups flour

½ cup minced parsley

½ cup seasoning salt

1 teaspoon cayenne pepper

20 ounces potato buds

2 tablespoons dry mustard

Combine all ingredients; mix well.

Walleye:

6 to 8 Walleye fillets

Egg wash

Dijon mustard

Cooked long grain or wild rice

Brush each walleye fillet with Dijon mustard. Dip in egg wash and then into potato crust mix. Press firmly to adhere. Heat sauté pan with butter over medium heat and sauté until golden brown. Serve walleye over rice and ladle cucumber sour cream dressing over the fillet. Serve with lemon wedge.

Troy Dox, Food & Beverage Director
Ruttger's Bay Lake Lodge

Walleye Cakes

2 pounds walleye, skinned and
   boned
1 tablespoon canola oil
1 yellow onion, chopped
1 red bell pepper, chopped
1 tablespoon chopped garlic
½ cup white wine
¼ cup butter
½ cup flour

1 tablespoon dry dill
1 tablespoon paprika
Salt and pepper to taste
1 tablespoon chopped parsley
5 eggs
2 cups flour
Salt and pepper to taste
½ pound seasoned breadcrumbs
Oil for frying

Sauté walleye over medium heat in oil. Break walleye up in pan with wooden spoon. Sauté 3 minutes, add onions and peppers and sauté 4 minutes. Add garlic and sauté 2 minutes. Add wine and cook until reduced by half. Add butter, stir and melt. Slowly add flour and stir as it thickens. When mixture is thick enough to hold shape, season with dill, paprika, salt, pepper and parsley. Cool 1 hour. Using a 1 ounce scoop, make balls with walleye mixture and flatten tops to make them into walleye cakes. Whisk eggs in 1 bowl, combine flour, salt and pepper in another bowl, and place breadcrumbs in final bowl. Place each walleye cake into seasoned flour, evenly coating each cake. Take floured cakes and place into egg wash and evenly coat each cake. Place right into breadcrumbs, coating evenly. Pour oil into frying pan 1 to 2 inches deep. Heat to 350° and cook each cake 4 to 5 minutes or until golden.

Delicious served with Rémoulade.

Visit Winona

Salmon Sandwich Bake

¼ to ½ cup soft butter (not melted)
2 teaspoons prepared mustard
12 pieces sliced bread
2 (7.75-ounce) cans salmon, drained
1 cup shredded cheese

1 small onion
1 (10.75-ounce) can cream of shrimp
   soup
¼ cup milk

Preheat oven to 350°. Combine butter and mustard. Toast bread and remove crusts. Spread butter mixture on 1 side of bread. Place 6 slices, buttered side up, in ungreased baking dish. Flake salmon and crush bones. Mix with cheese and onion. Spread salmon mixture evenly over bread in baking dish. Cut remaining 6 slices of bread diagonally in half. Place buttered side up on salmon mixture. Mix soup and milk, pour evenly on and around the sandwiches. Bake uncovered 25 minutes or until hot and bubbly.

Joanne Toinette Trenda, submitted by her daughter, Angel Pekarna
Taste of Shakopee

Bourbon Planked Salmon

Cedar Planks:
2 cups inexpensive bourbon
6 cups water
4 cedar planks

Combine liquid ingredients and pour over cedar planks. Soak minimum of 6 hours. Remove planks from liquid.

Sockeye Salmon:
4 (8-ounce) portions salmon
4 soaked cedar planks
Salt and pepper to taste
1 cup honey
4 tablespoons brown sugar, divided
4 tablespoons butter, divided

Place portions of salmon on each plank, skin side down and place on very hot grill. Lightly season salmon with salt and pepper and cook, covered, until inside juices begin to ooze from fillet. Brush entire exposed salmon with honey, top off with 1 tablespoon brown sugar and 1 tablespoon butter. Cover and allow glaze to melt together. Once glaze hits the grill it will ignite the cedar, continuing the smoking process. This only takes about 2 minutes. Extinguish fire and enjoy!

Tom Linderholm, Corporate Chef
Odyssey Resorts

Shrimp and Pea Rice Bowl

1 tablespoons extra-virgin olive oil
1 pound raw shrimp, peeled and deveined
3 tablespoons finely chopped shallots
4 garlic cloves, minced
1 cup frozen peas, cooked according to directions
1 tablespoon rice vinegar
½ teaspoon kosher salt
1 teaspoon crushed red pepper flakes
½ teaspoon ground turmeric
2 tablespoons fresh chopped parsley
4 cups brown rice, cooked

Heat oil in large skillet over medium-high heat. Add shrimp and shallots and sauté 2 minutes. Add garlic and sauté 1 minute until shrimp is done. Add peas, vinegar, salt, pepper flakes and turmeric. Cook until heated through. Sprinkle with parsley and serve over rice.

Culturfest

Kayaks at Appeldoorn's Sunset Bay Resort

Lemon Shrimp

1 (16-ounce) package angel hair pasta
2 tablespoons olive oil
3 tablespoons butter
1 can sliced black olives, drained
1 jar artichoke hearts, drained
4 ounces sliced mushrooms, drained
4 cloves garlic, finely chopped
1 teaspoon coarse pepper
2 lemons, zested and juiced
1 pound shrimp, peeled and deveined

Cook angel hair pasta according to package directions. In large skillet, combine olive oil and butter. Add olives, artichoke hearts, mushrooms, garlic, pepper, and lemon zest. Sauté 5 minutes. Add shrimp, ½ cup water from pasta and juice from lemons. Cook until shrimp is pink, 5 to 8 minutes depending on shrimp size. Serve shrimp over pasta.

Hyde-A-Way Bay Resort

Grilled Fish

¼ cup bottled honey-Dijon salad dressing
2 tablespoons Indian curry paste
2 tablespoons maple syrup
½ teaspoon salt
6 (8-ounce) tilapia, salmon or catfish fillets, preferably skinless

In a large bowl, stir dressing with curry paste, maple syrup and salt. Add fish and turn to evenly coat. Let stand at room temperature while heating grill. Lightly oil grill and heat to medium-high. Place fish on grill. Cook with lid closed 4 to 6 minutes, then brush tops with remaining marinade. Turn and continue grilling 3 to 8 more minutes, or until knife tip inserted into center comes out warm.

Dick Dahlen
Big Island Rendezvous

Quinoa with Fish

1 cup quinoa
2 cups water
1 teaspoon salt
2½ teaspoons extra-virgin olive oil, divided
1 pound boneless, skinless tilapia fillets, divided into 8 pieces
Coarse salt and ground pepper to taste
¾ teaspoon paprika
1 cup English cucumber, diced small
⅓ cup roughly chopped fresh dill
⅓ cup crumbled feta
2 teaspoons fresh lemon juice

In small saucepan, bring quinoa, water and 1 teaspoon salt to boil. Reduce to simmer and cook until water evaporates, about 15 minutes. Transfer quinoa to medium bowl and let cool 5 minutes. In large, nonstick skillet, heat 1½ teaspoons oil over medium-high. Pat fish dry and season with salt and pepper; sprinkle with paprika. Cook fillets until opaque throughout, about 4 minutes, flipping halfway through. Stir cucumber, dill, feta, 1 teaspoon oil and lemon juice into quinoa. Season with salt and pepper. Divide quinoa among four plates and top with fish.

Dick Dahlen
Big Island Rendezvous

Zesty Halibut

Zest of 3 lemons
2 tablespoons sugar
1 tablespoon salt
⅓ cup plus 1 teaspoon freshly squeezed lemon juice
3 tablespoons chopped fresh dill
4 (8-ounce) halibut fillets
1 tablespoon olive oil
3 tablespoons butter, cut into thirds

In a small bowl, combine lemon zest, sugar, salt, 1 tablespoon lemon juice and dill. Place fillets in shallow, nonreactive container. Cover with lemon-dill marinade and refrigerate 3 hours.

Remove fish and set marinade aside. Heat large sauté pan coated with olive oil. Sauté fillets until golden and cooked through, about 5 minutes per side. Remove from heat; transfer fillets to a platter. Cover with aluminum foil to keep warm. Turn heat to high; add reserved marinade. When bubbly and brown, add remaining lemon juice. Cook 1 minute. Reduce heat to low. Add butter, swirling pan to melt. Remove pan from heat. Pour sauce over fillets and serve.

Dick Dahlen
Big Island Rendezvous

Blackened Swordfish

Béarnaise Sauce:

2 sticks unsalted butter

4 shallots, finely chopped

2 tablespoons fresh tarragon leaves

4 white peppercorns, crushed

¼ cup white wine vinegar

⅓ cup dry white wine

4 large egg yolks

¼ teaspoon salt

Melt butter in medium saucepan over medium heat. Boil shallots, tarragon and peppercorns in vinegar and wine in a nonreactive medium-size saucepan over medium heat until reduced to about ¼ cup.

Strain into top of a double boiler. Whisk in egg yolks. Place top over bottom of double boiler containing simmering water. Make sure water is below the bottom of upper part. Whisk constantly.

As soon as yolk mixture begins to thicken slightly, remove the top of double boiler and continue whisking. Turn off heat. Add four ice cubes to bottom of double boiler to cool water. Put top with yolks back on. Whisk in melted butter very slowly. (If at any time the sauce looks as if it is about to break, remove top and continue whisking to cool or whisk in 1 teaspoon cold water.) Whisking constantly, add salt and cayenne. When butter is incorporated, taste and add more salt or cayenne as needed.

Swordfish Steaks:

2 ounces canola oil

2 (8-ounce) swordfish steaks

2 tablespoons Cajun seasoning

8 cups fresh spinach

2 ounces dry white wine

¼ teaspoon salt

¼ teaspoon pepper

8 ounces Béarnaise sauce

2 lemon wedges

Ladle oil onto 375° griddle. Season fish with Cajun spice; place in oil. Cook, flipping once, until an internal temperature of 145° has been achieved. Steam spinach with white wine, salt and pepper, making sure to not allow spinach to wilt. Place spinach in center of serving dish. Place fish on top of spinach; top with Béarnaise sauce. Garnish with lemon wedge.

Roseville Convention and Visitors Bureau

Beer Batter

1½ cups flour
½ teaspoon salt
3 eggs, beaten

3 teaspoons baking
    powder
1 cup beer

Blend all ingredients and use as batter for frying favorite foods.

Visit Brainerd

Fountains in Albert Lea

Best-Ever Brown Gravy

2 tablespoons oil
2 tablespoons flour
2 cups water
2 teaspoons beef bouillon
¼ teaspoon black pepper

¼ teaspoon Kitchen Bouquet
2 tablespoons butter
½ teaspoon garlic powder
⅛ teaspoon onion powder

Mix oil and flour in small bowl to make paste. Add more oil if too thick; set aside. Combine water, bouillon, pepper, Kitchen Bouquet, butter, garlic powder and onion powder in a large pot. Bring to a boil. Slowly add flour paste, stirring constantly. Continue boiling and stirring 2 to 3 minutes. Reduce heat and simmer 5 minutes. Remove from heat, gravy will thicken upon standing.

Sonshine Music Festival

July

Willmar
320-235-6723
www.sonshinefestival.com

Started in 1982, the Sonshine Music Festival has become a summer highlight for hundreds of thousands of people over the past 32 years. The four day festival includes the best in Christian music and speakers. The list of artists who have appeared at Sonshine is a 'who's who' of Christian musicians. Although Sonshine began as a youth event it has grown into an experience for the entire family. There is music and activities for every age. Camping is how most people enjoy Sonshine, although the area motels are great Sonshiner hosts. The Sonshine experience is rich in music and time with friends and family.

Chinese Brown Gravy

6 tablespoons flour
6 tablespoons drippings from
   roast beef, ham or chicken
2 tablespoons soy sauce
1 teaspoon brown gravy sauce

1 teaspoon salt
Dash pepper
½ cup cold water
1½ cups hot water

Blend flour with drippings. Add soy sauce, brown gravy sauce, salt, pepper and cold water; mix thoroughly. Stir in hot water. Cook until smooth and thickened, stirring constantly. Yield: 2 cups.

Culturfest

Thyme Mushroom Gravy

2 cups vegetable stock
⅓ cup dried mushrooms (mixed
   is good...fresh is fine, too!)
3 tablespoons butter
2 tablespoons minced shallot
1 clove garlic, minced (optional)

3 tablespoons flour
3 tablespoons soy sauce
½ cup light cream
1 tablespoon sherry
1 tablespoon minced fresh thyme
Salt and pepper to taste

Bring vegetable stock to boil. In a small bowl, pour stock over mushrooms. Soak 20 minutes. Remove mushrooms; set aside stock. Mince or thinly slice mushrooms; set aside. In medium saucepan, melt butter. Add shallot and garlic. Sauté 5 minutes over medium heat until softened. Add flour, cooking constantly; cook 2 minutes. Gradually add 1½ cups reserved vegetable stock, leaving mushroom sediment out, mixing well. Cook over medium heat until thickened. Add mushrooms, soy sauce, cream, sherry and thyme. Cook until heated through and thickened to desired consistency. Season with salt and pepper.

Serve with chopped sirloin and potatoes.

Culturfest

Marinade

¼ cup salad oil
¼ cup olive oil
½ cup low-sodium soy sauce
½ cup red wine vinegar
1 teaspoon crushed red
   pepper
1 teaspoon black pepper

1 teaspoon finely chopped
   parsley
1 tablespoon minced garlic
1 tablespoon minced onion
2 teaspoons garlic salt
¼ cup sugar

Combine all ingredients and mix well. This marinade is perfect for all types of meat. Marinate chicken and steaks overnight. Marinate shrimp 8 hours.

Tall Timber Days

North Country Basting Sauce

1 cup ketchup
⅔ cup apple cider vinegar
½ cup vegetable oil
1 tablespoon Worcestershire
   sauce

½ cup pure maple syrup
1 tablespoon Dijon mustard
½ teaspoon chili powder
½ teaspoon salt
¼ teaspoon cayenne pepper

Bring ingredients to a boil over medium heat, stirring occasionally. Reduce heat and cook 10 minutes, stirring occasionally. Cool and refrigerate. Use as a basting sauce for your favorite meat.

Audubon Center of the North Woods

Desserts & Other Sweets

Cinnamon Roll Cake

3 cups flour
¼ teaspoon salt
1 cup sugar
4 teaspoons baking powder

1½ cups milk
2 eggs, beaten
2 teaspoons vanilla
½ cup butter, melted

Combine flour, salt, sugar, baking powder, milk, eggs and vanilla; mix well. Slowly stir in butter and pour into greased 9x13-inch pan.

Topping:

1 cup butter, softened
1 cup brown sugar

2 tablespoons flour
1 tablespoon cinnamon

Combine all ingredients and mix well. Drop evenly over batter and swirl with knife. Bake at 350° for 28 to 32 minutes.

Glaze:

2 cups powdered sugar
5 tablespoons milk

1 teaspoon vanilla

Combine all ingredients. Drizzle over warm cake.

Taste Twin Cities

Streusel Coffee Cake

(Israel)

½ cup butter, softened
1 cup sugar
2 eggs
1 teaspoon vanilla

1 cup sour cream
2 cups flour
1 teaspoon baking powder
1 teaspoon baking soda

Cream together butter and sugar. Beat together eggs and vanilla. Combine butter mixture with egg mixture; add sour cream. Sift together flour, baking powder and baking soda. Combine with other ingredients. Spread half in a 9x13-inch greased pan.

Topping:

2 tablespoons butter, softened
2 tablespoons flour
1 teaspoon cinnamon

½ cup brown sugar
½ cup chopped nuts

Combine all ingredients and sprinkle ½ on top of mixture in pan. Spread remaining batter on top of this; sprinkle with remaining topping. Pat topping into dough. Bake at 350° for 45 minutes.

Culturfest

Taste Twin Cities

A Corner Cake (Wedding Cake)

1½ cups white sugar
½ cup shortening
½ cup boiling water
3 cups flour
3 teaspoons baking powder
½ teaspoon salt
½ cup sweet milk
3 egg whites, beaten stiff

Grease and flour 9x13-inch pan. Mix sugar and shortening; add boiling water. Sift flour, baking powder and salt together. Add dry ingredients alternately with milk. Fold in egg whites. Bake 30 to 40 minutes at 350°.

Amish Tours of Harmony

Snicker's Cake

1 package German chocolate cake mix
1 (14-ounce) package Kraft caramels
1 stick butter
¾ cup chocolate chips
1 cup chopped nuts (optional)

Prepare cake mix according to package directions. Pour ½ batter into greased 9x13-inch pan. Bake at 350° for 20 minutes. Meanwhile, melt caramels and butter in double boiler. Once cake has baked 20 minutes, remove from oven and pour caramel mixture over cake. Sprinkle chocolate chips and nuts over top of cake. Dot remaining batter on top of cake and return to oven. Bake 20 minutes at 250°, then at 350° for 10 to 15 minutes.

Appeldoorn's Sunset Bay Resort

English Raisin Cake

1 pound raisins	2 teaspoons baking soda
1½ cups sugar	3 teaspoons cinnamon
½ cup butter, softened	1 teaspoon nutmeg
2 eggs	⅛ pound citron
3 cups flour	½ cup chopped nuts

In saucepan, cover raisins with 2½ cups water and simmer until soft. Drain, reserving 1½ cups liquid for cake. Cream sugar and butter in a bowl. Add eggs, beating well. Sift together dry ingredients and add alternately with reserved liquid from raisins. Add raisins and nuts. Mix thoroughly. Pour into 9x13-inch baking dish. Bake 45 minutes at 375°.

Culturfest

Winona County Courthouse

5 Minute Chocolate Cake in a Mug

4 tablespoons flour
4 tablespoons sugar
2 tablespoons cocoa
1 egg
3 tablespoons milk
3 tablespoons oil
3 tablespoons chocolate chips (optional)
¼ teaspoon vanilla extract
1 large, microwavable mug

Combine flour, sugar and cocoa in mug; mix well. Add egg and mix. Add milk, oil, chocolate chips and vanilla; stir well. Place in microwave and cook 3 minutes at 1000 watts. Cake will rise over top of mug. Cool. Eat in cup or turn out onto plate.

Chickadee Boutique

S'mores Brownie Cake

Marshmallow:

1⅔ cups sugar
¾ cup light corn syrup
⅓ cup water

2 packets powdered gelatin
1 teaspoon vanilla extract
½ cup powdered sugar

Grease 9x13-inch pan. Combine sugar, corn syrup and water together in a saucepan and bring to 240°, stirring frequently. Add gelatin and corn syrup sauce to mixer. Using whip attachment, whip 5 minutes on medium-high speed, add vanilla and whip 1 minute. Scrape mixture out of bowl and place in greased pan. Sprinkle powdered sugar on top and refrigerate 2 hours.

Crust:

2 cups finely ground graham cracker
  crumbs

¾ cup sugar
½ cup butter, melted

Grease separate 9x13-inch pan; set aside. Combine dry ingredients in large bowl. Melt butter and add to dry ingredients. Mix thoroughly. Press evenly into pan.

Cake:

⅓ pound butter, softened
1½ cups sugar
2 eggs
1½ cups flour
1 teaspoon baking soda

3 tablespoons cocoa powder
⅓ cup buttermilk
⅓ cup sour cream
1 teaspoon vanilla extract

Preheat oven to 350°. Cream butter and sugar together until light and fluffy. Add eggs and mix until thoroughly combined. In a small mixing bowl, sift flour, baking soda and cocoa powder together; set aside. In separate, small mixing bowl, whisk buttermilk, sour cream and vanilla together.

Add dry ingredients in 3 batches, alternating with the liquid ingredients. Pour batter on top of graham crust and bake 30 minutes. Place in refrigerator to cool.

Chocolate Ganache:

9 ounces chocolate chips

1 cup heavy cream

Place mixture in double boiler and whisk until smooth.

Pour evenly over brownie cake while the ganache is still warm. Carefully place marshmallow on top of cake, cool and cut.

Tom Linderholm, Corporate Chef
Odyssey Resorts

Pound Cake for Choco-holics

1 cup butter, softened
½ cup shortening
3 cups sugar
5 eggs
3 cups flour, sifted

½ teaspoon baking powder
½ teaspoon salt
½ cup cocoa
1 cup milk
1 teaspoon vanilla

Preheat oven to 325°. Cream together butter, shortening, and sugar until smooth. Add eggs, 1 at a time, beating well after each. In a separate bowl, combine flour, baking powder, salt and cocoa; mix well. Alternately add dry mixture and milk to butter mixture. Stir in vanilla. Pour into greased and floured 10-inch tube pan. Bake 1 hour and 20 minutes or until toothpick inserted near center comes out clean. Delicious served warm with ice cream.

Edgewater Hotel and Waterpark

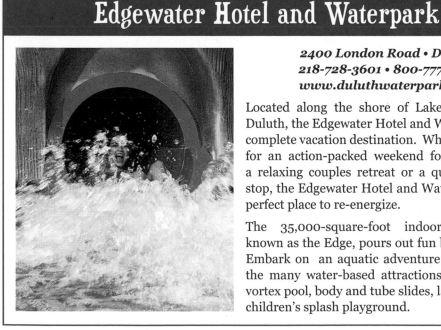

Chocolate Mazurek
(Mazurek Czekoladowy)

½ cup butter, softened
1 cup sugar
½ cup melted baking chocolate
4 eggs, lightly beaten

1 teaspoon vanilla extract
Salt to taste
1 tablespoon milk
2 cups flour

Cream together butter and sugar; add melted chocolate slowly. Add eggs, vanilla, salt and milk; mix well. Gradually sift in flour. Spread evenly on a greased cookie sheet and bake 15 to 20 minutes at 350°.

White Icing:
2 tablespoons rum or lemon
   juice

1 cup powdered sugar
Grated nuts

Combine rum or lemon juice and powdered sugar; mix well. When cake is cool, drizzle with White Icing and top with grated nuts of your choice.

Twin Cities Polish Festival

Cream Cheese Frosting

1 (8-ounce) package cream cheese, softened
4 tablespoons butter (no substitutions), softened
5 cups powdered sugar
2 teaspoons pure vanilla

Cream together cream cheese and butter. Gradually add sugar and vanilla. Mix until smooth. Spread on favorite cake and enjoy!

Jeraldine Gustavson
Stand Still Parade

Black Bottom Cupcakes

1 (8-ounce) package cream
   cheese, softened
1 egg
⅓ cup sugar
Dash of salt
1 cup chocolate chips
1½ cups flour
¼ cup baking cocoa

⅓ cup cooking oil
1 teaspoon vanilla
1 cup sugar
1 teaspoon baking soda
1 cup water
1 tablespoon vinegar
½ teaspoon salt

In small bowl, cream together cream cheese, egg, sugar, salt and chocolate chips. Set aside. Combine remaining ingredients in large mixing bowl. Beat until well combined. Fill paper-lined muffin cups ⅓ full of cocoa batter. Top each one with a heaping teaspoon of cream cheese mixture. Sprinkle each cupcake with sugar and some chopped nuts. Bake at 350° for 20 to 25 minutes.

Joan Johnson
Stand Still Parade

Miniature Blueberry Cheesecakes

1 (8-ounce) package cream cheese,
  softened
¾ cup sugar
2 teaspoons finely grated lemon zest

1 teaspoon vanilla extract
1 pint blueberries
24 vanilla wafer cookies

Place cream cheese, sugar, zest and vanilla in food processor and pulse to combine. Add blueberries and pulse until mixed. Cut 24 small rounds of waxed paper and place each in bottom of 24-cup miniature muffin tin. Divide blueberry mixture among cups, spooning mixture on top of waxed paper. Place 1 vanilla wafer, flat side up, on top of batter in each cup, pressing gently to adhere. Cover with plastic and refrigerate overnight. To remove cheesecakes, run a warm, thin knife around each, then slide tip of knife under and lift out.

Little Falls Convention and Visitors Bureau

Little Falls

1-800-325-5916 • 1-320-616-4959
www.littlefallsmn.com

Established in 1848 on the banks of the mighty Mississippi River, Little Falls is one of the oldest cities in the state. Located in central Minnesota at the junction of Highway 10, 27, and 371, it was the "little falls" that attracted traders and explores. Today, Little Falls is still attracting businesses and travelers with many historical sites as well as scenic and recreational opportunities for nature and sports enthusiasts.

From Charles A. Lindbergh boyhood home to the downtown National Historic District, to golfing, biking, camping, fishing, snowmobiling, and special events. Take time to view the outdoor murals, visit a museum and enjoy a specialty coffee in a delightful café or on a sidewalk bakery/deli.

Experience the longest continuous trail with 3,000 miles of enjoyment.

Call the Little Falls Convention and Visitors Bureau for a custom tour.

Rhubarb Cake

2 cups rhubarb
1½ cups sugar
½ cup shortening
1 cup half-and-half
2 cups flour

1 egg
1 teaspoon baking soda
1 teaspoon vanilla
½ cup brown sugar
¼ teaspoon cinnamon

Mix rhubarb, sugar, shortening, half-and-half, flour, egg, baking soda and vanilla. Pour into greased and floured 9x13-inch pan. Sprinkle with brown sugar and cinnamon. Bake at 350° for 40 to 45 minutes.

Visit Brainerd

Easy Strawberry Cake

1 package white cake mix, plus ingredients to prepare per
 directions on box
1 cup strawberry preserves
⅛ teaspoon red food coloring
Cool Whip
Fresh strawberries

Prepare white cake according to package directions, but reduce
liquid called for by ⅓ cup and add strawberry preserves and
red food coloring. Bake 2 (9-inch) layers according to package
temperatures and time. When cake is cool, top each layer with
Cool Whip and strawberries. Makes 2 single layer cakes.

Pleasant Valley Orchard

Country Sampler Picnic

The Country Sampler Picnic is a
Brainerd original. Hosted at
the Northland Arboretum
this event entertains locals
and visitors alike with live
music, pig races, bouncy
races, and more.
Venders serve up
Minnesota produced
food, beer, and wine to
enjoy while enjoying
everything that this
event has to offer.

For more information
check out www.northlandarb.org

Strawberry Short Cake

1½ pounds strawberries, washed, stemmed and quartered
4 tablespoons sugar, divided
2 cups flour
2 teaspoons baking powder
¼ teaspoon baking soda
¾ teaspoon salt
1½ cups heavy cream
Whipped Cream (recipe follows)

Mix strawberries with 2 tablespoons sugar and refrigerate 30 minutes, allowing strawberries to create a juice. Preheat oven to 400°. Sift together flour, baking powder, baking soda, remaining 2 tablespoons sugar and salt in medium bowl. Add heavy cream and mix until just combined. Place mixture in an ungreased 8-inch square pan and bake 18 to 20 minutes or until golden. Remove shortcake from pan and place on rack to cool. Cut into 6 pieces and split each piece in half. Using ½ of the strawberries, spoon them and their juice onto each shortcake bottom. Top with dollop of whipped cream and place shortcake top. Spoon more strawberries over top and serve.

Whipped Cream:

1½ cups heavy cream, chilled
2 tablespoons sugar
1½ teaspoons vanilla extract
1 teaspoon freshly grated lemon zest (optional)

Using an electric mixer, beat heavy cream, sugar, vanilla and lemon zest 1½ to 2 minutes or until soft peaks form.

Wabasha Street Caves

Fresh Apple Cake

4 cups diced apples	1 cup chopped walnuts or pecans
2 eggs	2 cups unbleached flour
2 cups sugar	2 teaspoons baking soda
2 teaspoons cinnamon	1 teaspoon salt
½ cup salad oil	

Put diced apples in bowl, add eggs, mix 2 minutes by hand. Add sugar, cinnamon, oil and nuts. Mix well. In separate bowl, sift flour, baking soda and salt. Add flour mixture to apple mixture. Mix well. Pour mixture in 9x13-inch pan. Bake at 350° for 45 minutes.

Frosting:

½ cup butter, softened	1 teaspoon vanilla
1 egg	1 tablespoon milk (optional)
2 cups sugar	

Cream together butter and egg; add sugar and vanilla. Beat until smooth. Add milk if frosting is too stiff. Frost when cake is completely cool.

Bonnie Deardorff
Deardorff Orchards and Vineyards

Norwegian Apple Pie

½ cup brown sugar
2 tablespoons margarine
1 teaspoon baking powder
½ cup chopped nuts
½ teaspoon vanilla
¼ teaspoon salt
½ cup flour
1 cup chopped apples

Combine all ingredients. Mix well. Bake 30 minutes in greased pie pan at 350°.

Culturfest

Harvest Apple Pie

¾ cup sugar
½ teaspoon ground cinnamon
½ teaspoon ground nutmeg
¼ cup flour
Dash salt
6 cups cored, peeled and thinly sliced apples
2 (9-inch) pie crusts (top and bottom crust)
2 tablespoons butter

Preheat oven to 425°. Mix sugar, cinnamon, nutmeg, flour and salt. Stir in apples. Place mixture into pie crust, dot with butter. Cover with top crust and slit evenly to let steam escape. Seal top crust to bottom by pinching edges together. Cover edge of crust with 3- inch strip of aluminum foil. Bake 40 to 50 minutes, until crust is brown and juice begins to bubble through top. Serve topped with whipped cream or ice cream.

Key's Café All American Apple Pie

Crust:

1 cup shortening	⅓ cup water
2 cups flour	Dash salt
1 egg	Dash vinegar

Preheat oven to 375°. In a large bowl, combine all ingredients; mix well. Refrigerate 20 minutes.

Filling:

3 tablespoons flour	3 cups chopped apples
1 cup sugar	1 freshly squeezed lemon
½ teaspoon brown sugar	

In a large bowl, combine flour and sugars. Add apples. Squeeze lemon into mixture. When crust is cooled, divide it into two, equal halves. Roll one half out until it is ⅛-inch thick. Place in pie pan.

With a fork, poke holes in bottom of crust. Place filling into pie pan. Roll out remaining pie dough and place on top, sealing edges. Bake 1 hour or until top is golden brown.

Roseville Convention and Visitors Bureau

Basic Pie Crust

2 cups flour
½ teaspoon salt
8 tablespoons lard
6 tablespoons ice water

Combine flour and salt. Cut in lard with pastry blender. Add water, form into ball. Roll out into 2 crusts.

Maggie Gergen, The Aroma Pie Shop
Stand Still Parade

Buttermilk Pie

½ cup sugar
2 tablespoons butter
1 egg, beaten
1 tablespoon flour
½ teaspoon baking soda
1 cup buttermilk
¼ teaspoon vanilla
1 unbaked pie shell
Cinnamon to taste

Cream sugar and butter; add egg. Combine flour and baking soda and add to butter mixture. Add buttermilk and vanilla. Pour onto pie crust and sprinkle with cinnamon. Bake at 350° for 35 minutes.

Amish Tours of Harmony

Pecan Apple Pie

1½ cups pecans
1 stick butter, melted
1 cup brown sugar

6 cups sliced apples
Sprinkle of cinnamon
1 prepared pie crust dough

Line bottom of pie plate with pecans. Pour butter over pecans. Top with brown sugar. Add sliced apples and sprinkle with cinnamon.

Cover with single pie crust. Bake at 375° for 50 to 55 minutes. Let sit 5 minutes and turn it over for an upside down apple pie.

Submitted by the Polish Museum
Visit Winona

Winona - Historic Island City

800-657-4972 • www.visitwinona.com

With the Mississippi River on one side of town and majestic limestone bluffs on the other, a more beautiful place than Winona is hard to find. This charming city—located in the Southeastern part of the state—is home to historically significant buildings, as well as a variety of dining, shopping, and lodging options, and numerous recreational opportunities. Winona has earned a reputation as an art and cultural mecca also, with several museums, a vineyard, and interesting festivals taking place throughout the year. Annual events like Taste of Winona offer food samples from local restaurants and Polish Apple Day is a Fall harvest festival featuring Polish cuisine and a variety of home baked apple goods. Don't miss Bloedow Bakery which was voted best doughnut shop in Minnesota in 2012 or the Lakeview Drive-Inn, Winona's oldest restaurant, where you can quench your thirst with a frosty mug of homemade root beer.

Shoo-Fly Pie

Base Mix:

12 cups flour

4 cups brown sugar

2 cups shortening

Pinch of salt

Mix together till a pie-crust type dough forms. Store in tight container.

Pie:

¾ cup molasses

¾ cups hot water

1 teaspoon baking soda

3 cups Base Mix, divided

Blend molasses, hot water and baking soda. Add 2 cups Base Mix. Pour in 9x9-inch pan. Sprinkle 1 cup Base Mix crumbs on top. Bake 30 to 40 minutes at 350°.

Amish Tours of Harmony

Nickle Dickle Day

No Crust Pumpkin Pie

1 (15-ounce) can pumpkin
½ teaspoon salt
1 (12-ounce) can evaporated
   skim milk

3 teaspoons pumpkin pie spice
3 egg whites
1 teaspoon vanilla
⅔ cup Splenda

Combine all ingredients and beat until smooth. Spray 9-inch pie plate with cooking spray and pour in mixture. Bake at 400° for 15 minutes, then 325° for an additional 45 minutes or until knife inserted comes out clean.

Center Creek Orchard

Pumpkin Cream Cheese Pie

1½ cups crushed vanilla wafers
¼ cup melted butter
1 (8-ounce) package cream
   cheese, softened
3 eggs, divided

¾ cup sugar, divided
1¼ cups canned pumpkin
1 cup evaporated milk
1 teaspoon pumpkin pie spice
Whipped cream for serving

Mix wafer crumbs and butter. Press into bottom and up sides of 9-inch pie pan. Beat cream cheese, 1 egg and ¼ cup sugar until smooth. Spread on top of crust. Mix remaining eggs and sugar, pumpkin, milk and pumpkin spice. Carefully pour over top of cream cheese. Crust will be full. Bake at 350° for 1 hour or until set. Cool. Serve topped with whipped cream.

Center Creek Orchard

Butterfinger Cream Pie

1 (8-ounce) package cream cheese, softened
1 (8-ounce) carton Cool Whip
4 ounces Butterfinger pieces, crushed
1 (9-inch) graham cracker pie crust

In small mixing bowl, beat cream cheese until smooth. Fold in
Cool Whip. Crush candy bars into pieces and fold in mixture.
Spoon into pie crust. Top with more crushed candy bar pieces.
Cool in refrigerator and cut into 8 pieces.

Executive Chef Terry Dox
Ruttger's Bay Lake Lodge

Ruttger's Bay Lake Lodge

25039 Tame Fish Lake Road
Deerwood
218-678-2885 • 800-450-4545
www.ruttgers.com

Ruttger's Bay Lake Lodge is a Minnesota
lake resort that features cottages, villas,
condominiums and guestrooms, varied
restaurant and bar options, spa, golf, tennis,
pools, beach and lake activities, a full service
marina, supervised children's program,
nature program and planned activities,
plus a conference center equipped to serve
meetings and events of all sizes. The Ruttger
family opened the resort in 1898 and gained
a reputation for friendly service in a beautiful
setting. Five generations later, they are still
here treating every guest just like family.
Welcome to the lake!

Chocolate Cobbler

2 sticks butter
2¼ cups sugar, divided
1½ cups self-rising flour
1 teaspoon vanilla
¾ cup milk
6 tablespoons cocoa powder
2 cups boiling water

Preheat oven to 350°. Place butter in 9x13-inch glass baking dish and melt in oven. In a medium bowl, combine 1¼ cups sugar, flour, vanilla and milk. When butter is melted pour batter over butter, but do not stir. In a separate bowl combine cocoa and remaining 1 cup sugar.

Sprinkle cocoa/sugar mixture on top of batter. Do not stir. Pour boiling water on top of cocoa/sugar mixture; do not stir. Bake 30 to 45 minutes. Serve warm. Delicious topped with ice cream.

Dick Dahlen
Big Island Rendezvous

Rhubarb Crunch

Crust:

2 cups flour	1 cup butter
2 cups brown sugar	2 cups quick oats

Combine all ingredients, mixing well. Gently pat half of mixture into greased 9x13-inch pan. Save remainder of mixture for topping.

Filling:

6 cups diced rhubarb	2 tablespoons cornstarch
1 cup sugar	1 cup water

Spoon diced rhubarb over crust in baking dish. In saucepan, mix sugar and cornstarch. Stir in water. Cook until clear and thickened. Pour over rhubarb. Top with remaining crust mixture. Bake at 350° for 50 minutes.

The Left Bank Café
City of Slayton

City of Slayton

507-836-8534
www.slayton.govoffice.com

The City of Slayton and the Slayton Chamber of Commerce would like visitors to know about all the fantastic businesses in the city. This is evident in the Chamber's mission statement: *To Welcome, Inform, Protect, and Educate Business Organizations and Individuals about Opportunities in the Slayton Area. To Promote Civic Interests and General Welfare of Slayton and Surrounding Area.*"

Bear Paw Resort's Rhubarb Crunch

Crust:
1½ cups flour
1¼ cups quick oats
1½ cups packed brown sugar
1½ teaspoons cinnamon
¾ cup melted butter

Combine all ingredients. Mix until crumbly and press half of mixture into ungreased 9x13-inch pan. Set aside remaining crumb mixture

Filling:
6 cups chopped rhubarb
1½ cups sugar
3 tablespoons cornstarch
1½ cups water
1½ teaspoon vanilla

Pour rhubarb over crumb crust; set aside. Combine sugar, cornstarch and water in saucepan and cook over medium-high heat, stirring until bubbly. Continue to cook and stir 2 minutes. Remove from heat and add vanilla. Pour over rhubarb. Top with remaining crumb mixture. Bake at 350° for 50 minutes or until bubbly.

Joel Hays, owner
Bear Paw Resort

Almond Butter Crunch

1 cup butter
1⅓ cups sugar
1 tablespoon light corn syrup
3 tablespoons water

1 teaspoon vanilla
1 cup coarsely chopped toasted
   almonds
1 large Hershey Bar

Melt butter in heavy pan. Add sugar, corn syrup and water. Stir frequently and cook to 300°. Watch closely after it reaches 275°, it will burn quickly. Remove from heat, stir in vanilla and nuts. Pour into ungreased 9x13-inch pan. Break up Hershey bar and lay on top. Spread when melted. Let stand until set and chocolate is hardened. Break into pieces.

Tips:

• May sprinkle finely chopped toasted almonds on chocolate before it is set.

• Toasted pecans are a great variation from the almonds.

• It is best to cook over medium heat rather than quickly over high heat.

Gail Lundgren
Agate Days Celebration

Apple Oatmeal Crisp

3 or 4 tart cooking apples, peeled, cored and thinly sliced
½ cup butter, melted
¾ cup firmly packed brown sugar
¾ cup quick oats
½ cup flour
1 teaspoon powdered cinnamon

Arrange apples in greased shallow baking dish; set aside. In separate bowl, add butter and stir in sugar, oats, flour and cinnamon until well mixed. Sprinkle over apples. Bake 350° for 45 minutes or until crust is golden brown and apples are soft. Serve warm with whipped cream, vanilla ice cream or Cheddar cheese.

Center Creek Orchard

Fall Festival at Center Creek Orchard

63 254th Avenue • Fairmont
507-773-4547 • www.centercreekorchard.com

Center Creek Orchard invites guests to come and experience the Fall Festival. Their goal is to provide visitors with apples that are freshly picked and a day full of fun in a family atmosphere. Activities include hayrides, storytelling, corn pile, scarecrow building, castle bouncer, a giant maze, apple sling, barrel ride, crawling tunnels, a super slide and haunted forest. Guests may pick their own pumpkin from the pumpkin patch and select apples from over a dozen Minnesota varieties. Admission is $7.00 per person for the festival, there is no admission charge to the apple barn and picnic areas. The miniature golf course is outside the festival area and only $3.00 per person.

Apple Crisp for a Crowd

5 pounds canned apple pie
    filling
7 pounds apples, peeled and
    sliced
2½ cups quick oats

3¾ cups brown sugar
2½ cups flour
3¾ teaspoons cinnamon
3¾ teaspoons nutmeg
3 sticks butter

Place apples and pie filling in large roaster. Combine oats, brown sugar, flour, cinnamon and nutmeg. Melt butter and add to oat mixture until moist and crumbly. Sprinkle mixture over apples. Bake at 350° for 45 minutes until bubbly and golden brown. Serve with favorite vanilla ice cream

Gibbs Museum

Apple Festival

First weekend in October

The heritage apple orchard at Gibbs Museum is one of the only orchards of its type in the Midwest. With apple varieties dating to Jefferson and Franklin's time, the orchard also has trees that are the grandparents of famous Minnesota apples such as the Honey Crisp. Inspired by the orchard, the annual Apple Festival includes apple tasting, horse-drawn hayrides, a hay maze, apple crafts, apple games and apple food, all in the beautiful setting of the Gibbs farm.

Apfelstrudel (Apple Strudel)

2½ cups flour
1½ cups sugar, plus 1 tablespoon
1 teaspoon salt
1 cup shortening
2 egg, separated

Milk
1½ cups corn flakes, crumbled
1 teaspoon cinnamon
8 to 10 apples, pared and sliced
    thin

Sift together flour, 1 tablespoon sugar, and salt; cut in shortening. Put egg yolks in measuring cup; add enough milk to make ⅔ cup liquid. Roll out ½ dough for 12x15-inch cookie sheet. Sprinkle corn flakes over dough. In medium bowl, add cinnamon and remaining sugar to apples. Place apples over corn flakes; roll out remaining dough and place on top. Seal edges. Beat egg whites until frothy, spread over top. Bake at 400° for 10 minutes or until brown; reduce heat and bake at 350° for 45 minutes. Remove from oven and dribble powdered sugar frosting over top.

Powdered Sugar Frosting:

⅔ cup powdered sugar
Milk

½ teaspoon vanilla

Combine all ingredients, adding enough milk to make consistency good for drizzling.

Culturfest

Apple Delight

2 cups flour
2 cups butter
1 ¾ cups sugar, divided
Salt
1 teaspoon cinnamon
Pinch nutmeg
12 apples, peeled, cored and sliced
2 eggs, separated
2 cups milk
2 tablespoons cornstarch
1 teaspoon vanilla

Combine flour, butter, 2 tablespoons sugar and pinch of salt. Pat onto 9x13-inch cake pan. Mix 1 cup sugar, cinnamon and nutmeg with sliced apples and place on crust. Bake 1 hour at 350°. While baking, make custard by combining beaten egg yolks, milk, cornstarch, 2 tablespoons sugar and pinch of salt. Cook in saucepan until thick and let cool. Pour over baked apples and spread. Beat egg whites and add ½ cup sugar and vanilla. Place on top of custard. Return to oven and brown the meringue.

A maze'n Farmyard

Deardorff Apple Crisp

Topping:

½ cup butter, melted	½ cup brown sugar
1 cup flour	½ teaspoon vanilla
½ cup sugar	¼ teaspoon ground coriander

Combine all ingredients; mix well and set aside.

Filling:

6 to 8 apples, peeled, cored and chopped	½ cup sugar
	½ teaspoon cinnamon

Stir together apples, sugar and cinnamon. Pour into 9x13-inch baking pan. Spread topping mixture over apples. Bake at 425° for 20 minutes. Lower temperature to 350° and bake 20 minutes.

Bonnie Deardorff
Nickle Dickle Day

Nickle Dickle Day
2nd Saturday after Labor Day

Waconia
www.DestinationWaconia.org
952-442-5812

Over 50 years ago, Waconia business owners got together and created this day to attract people from the area to town for bargains and fun contests. That is still true today. This is a day for shopping, fun and catching up with friends, family and neighbors – a true town festival. Join the fun in downtown Waconia at City Square Park and all around for a variety of events like the car show, 3 on 3 basketball tournament, fun runs, live music in the park, a craft fair and great food. Visitors can also ride a mechanical bull – no matter how young or old they are. For the civic minded, there are Rotary Duck Races and the Public Library Book Sale fundraiser. The shops feature great deals and showcase the small town charm of this one day event sponsored by the Waconia Chamber of Commerce.

Maple Apple Crisp

Sliced apples are slathered in syrup, covered with a wonderful crumble, baked and served warm with scoops of rum raisin ice cream.

5 apples (peeled, cored and sliced)
¾ cup pure maple syrup
½ cup flour
½ cup old-fashioned oats

½ cup brown sugar
1 pinch salt
½ cup softened butter

Preheat oven to 375°. Place apples in 8x8-inch baking dish. Toss apples with syrup. In a separate bowl, mix together flour, oats, sugar and salt. Cut in butter until mixture is crumbly. Sprinkle mixture evenly over apples. Bake 35 minutes, until topping is golden brown. Serve warm or at room temperature.

Audubon Center of the North Woods

The Syruping Day

Sometimes winter may seem long, but before you know it, those cold, snowy days give way to warmer, longer days – that's when the sap begins flowing in the many maple trees at the Audubon Center of the North Woods. That's maple syrup time! Every year, the Center hosts its annual Maple Syrup Day – a delicious pancake brunch followed by a hands-on program that covers all aspects of maple syruping.

Learn which trees in the woods are maple trees, along with the history and process of making maple syrup. Actively participate in all the phases of syrup-making including tapping maple trees, collecting sap, and observing the sap being boiled down into liquid gold maple syrup. Space is limited and reservations are required.

Pumpkin Dessert

1 (18.25 ounce) package yellow cake mix, divided
⅓ cup butter, melted
4 eggs, divided
1 (29-ounce) can pumpkin
½ cup brown sugar
⅔ cup milk
2 tablespoons pumpkin pie spice
½ cup butter, chilled
½ cup sugar
¾ cup chopped walnuts

Preheat oven to 350° and lightly grease 9x13-inch baking dish. Set aside 1 cup cake mix. Combine remaining cake mix with melted butter and 1 egg and mix until well blended; spread mixture in bottom of prepared baking dish. In a large bowl, combine pumpkin, brown sugar, milk, 3 eggs and pumpkin pie spice; mix well and pour over cake mix mixture in baking dish. With an electric mixer, combine chilled butter, white sugar and reserved cake mix until mixture resembles coarse crumbs. Sprinkle over pumpkin mixture. Sprinkle chopped walnuts over all. Bake 45 to 50 minutes, until top is golden.

Audubon Center of the North Woods

Audubon Center of the North Woods

54165 Audubon Drive,
Located on the east side of Grindstone Lake near Sandstone
888-404-7743 • www.audubon-center.org

The Audubon Center of the North Woods is a private, non-profit residential environmental learning and conference and retreat center on the shores of Grindstone Lake near Sandstone in the east-central part of the state. The diverse 535-acre lakeside sanctuary includes a variety of habitats, including old-growth red and white pines, hardwood forests, restored wetlands and prairies. This unique center features a mixture of historic and newly constructed facilities. There are many options available for guests, including lodging for up to 160 participants, wonderful meal service for 200+ in the beautiful lakeside dining hall, a wide variety of meeting spaces, and team-building, challenge or naturalist programs for any size group. In addition to being a field trip destination for schools, a field campus for several colleges, and hosting groups and conferences, the Center offers programs such as Women's Wellness & Adventure Weekends, Dinners at the Lake, Maple Syrup Day, and Winter Family Escape, just to name a few.

Oatmeal Carmelitas

Crust:

2 cups flour	1 teaspoon baking soda
2 cups quick oats	½ teaspoon salt
1½ cups brown sugar	1¼ cup butter, softened

Preheat oven to 350°. Grease 9x13-inch pan. In large bowl, blend all crust ingredients and mix at low speed until crumbly. Press half of crumb mixture, about 3 cups, in bottom of greased pan. Reserve remaining crumb mixture for topping. Bake 10 minutes.

Filling:

1 cup caramel ice cream topping	½ cup chopped nuts
3 tablespoons flour	8 Famous General Store of
1 (6-ounce) package semi-sweet chocolate chips	Minnetonka caramels, cut into 4 pieces each

In small bowl, combine caramel topping and flour. Remove partially baked crust from oven; sprinkle with chocolate chips, nuts and caramels. Drizzle caramel mixture on top, then sprinkle with reserved crumb mixture. Bake at 350° for 18 to 22 minutes or until golden brown. Cool completely. Refrigerate 1 to 2 hours until filling is set. Cut into bars.

General Store of Minnetonka

Snickerdoodle Bars

Batter:

¾ cup butter, softened
1¼ cups sugar
½ cup brown sugar
3 eggs

1 teaspoon vanilla
1¼ teaspoons baking powder
½ teaspoon salt
2⅓ cups flour

Preheat oven to 350°. Grease 9x13-inch baking pan; set aside. Combine all ingredients, mix well. Spoon ½ batter into pan; spread evenly.

Cinnamon Filling:

1 tablespoon sugar

1 tablespoon cinnamon

Combine sugar and cinnamon, sprinkle evenly over batter. Drop teaspoon-size amounts of remaining batter over filling.

Bake 20 to 25 minutes or until toothpick inserted in center comes out completely. Cool bars completely, about 1 hour.

Glaze (optional):

1 cup powdered sugar
1 to 2 tablespoons milk

¼ teaspoon vanilla

Combine all ingredients and drizzle over bars.

Kristie Swenson
Trimont FunFest

O'Henry Bars

1 cup butter
1 cup brown sugar
½ cup white corn syrup
4 cups quick oats

6 ounces chocolate chips
6 ounces butterscotch chips
½ cup peanut butter

Cream butter, brown sugar, corn syrup and oats in large bowl at low speed. Spread into greased 10x15-inch jelly roll pan. Bake at 350° for 12 minutes. Let set until cool. Place chips and peanut butter in saucepan and melt, watching carefully not to burn. Spread over bars and chill. Cut to desired size.

Culturfest

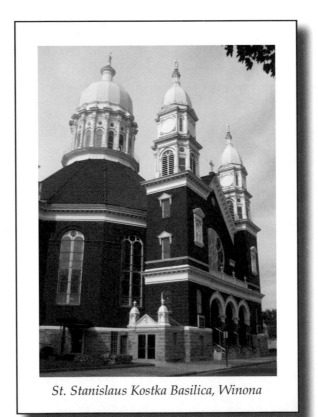

St. Stanislaus Kostka Basilica, Winona

Peanut Butter Squares

1 cup butter
1½ cups powdered sugar
1 cup peanut butter
2 cups graham cracker crumbs
2 cups chocolate chips

Combine butter, sugar, peanut butter and graham cracker crumbs and pat into 9x13-inch pan. Melt chocolate chips and spread over mixture; cut and chill.

R&M Amish Tours

Peanut Butter Fingers

¾ cup butter, softened	1½ teaspoons baking soda
¾ cup white sugar	¾ teaspoon vanilla
¾ cup brown sugar	1 cup flour
2 eggs	1 cup quick oats
½ cup peanut butter	6 ounces chocolate chips

Preheat oven to 350°. Cream together butter and sugars. Add eggs, peanut butter, baking soda and vanilla, mixing well. Add flour and oats gradually. Spread into greased 9x13-inch pan. Bake 10 to 15 minutes. Remove from oven and sprinkle with chocolate chips.

Topping:

½ cup powdered sugar	4 tablespoons milk
½ cup peanut butter	

Combine powdered sugar, peanut butter and milk; mix well, mixture will be very thick. Chocolate chips will have melted, spread chocolate evenly over cake. Drizzle with peanut butter mixture.

Hyde-A-Way Bay Resort

Special K Bars

1 cup sugar
1 cup corn syrup
1 cup creamy peanut butter
6 cups Special K cereal

½ (12-ounce) package
  chocolate chips
½ (12-ounce) package
  butterscotch chips

Combine sugar and corn syrup in large saucepan, heat to boiling. Remove from heat and add peanut butter. Mix until well melted. Add cereal and mix until well coated. Pour mixture into 9x13-inch pan and press down evenly. Melt chocolate and butterscotch chips, stir and pour over bars. Cool before serving.

Cara Sinn
Trimont Fun Fest

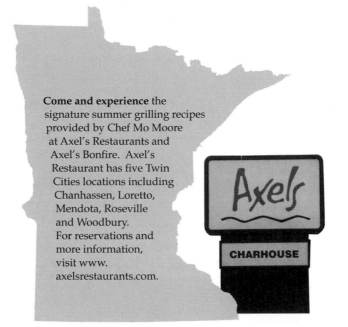

Come and experience the signature summer grilling recipes provided by Chef Mo Moore at Axel's Restaurants and Axel's Bonfire. Axel's Restaurant has five Twin Cities locations including Chanhassen, Loretto, Mendota, Roseville and Woodbury. For reservations and more information, visit www. axelsrestaurants.com.

Wild Rice Krispy Bars

Hand-parched wild lake rice is required. Do not expect fluffy kernels like popcorn. Wild lake rice pops into tiny, squiggly forms. It has a rich, nutty taste and wonderful crunch. Wild rice pops very quickly, in under 5 seconds, so be careful.

Vegetable oil
8 to 10 cups popped wild rice

1 stick butter
10 ounces marshmallows

To pop rice, fill an 8-inch skillet ⅔ full with oil. Heat until almost boiling, but not smoking. It is ready when a kernel of rice dropped into hot oil pops. Put ¼ cup or less wild rice into bottom of 6-inch wire mesh strainer and immerse into hot oil 2 to 5 seconds, or until all rice is popped. Drain in paper towel-lined container. Continue until desired amount of rice is reached.

Melt butter in 10-inch cooking pot over low heat. Add marshmallows and stir until completely melted. Add popped wild rice and stir into marshmallow mix until well coated. Grease a 12x16-inch pan. Using a greased spatula, press mixture evenly into. Cut into squares when cool.

Rick Smith, Director, American Indian Learning Resource Center

Buckeye Brownies

1 (19.5-ounce) package brownie mix, plus ingredients to prepare
   per directions on box
½ cup butter, melted
2 cups powdered sugar
1 cup creamy peanut butter
6 ounces semi-sweet chocolate chips
6 tablespoons butter

Prepare brownie mix according to package directions, using a greased 9x13-inch pan. Combine butter, powdered sugar and peanut butter; mix well. Spread over cooled brownies. Chill 1 hour. In saucepan, combine chocolate chips and butter and cook over low heat, stirring occasionally, until chocolate is melted. Spread over brownies.

Sue Strobel, guest
Bear Paw Resort

Cinderella Carriage at Center Creek Orchard

Black & White Cookies

1 cup unsalted butter
1¾ cups sugar
4 eggs
1 cup milk
½ teaspoon vanilla extract
¼ teaspoon lemon extract
2½ cups cake flour
2½ cups all-purpose flour
1 teaspoon baking powder
½ teaspoon salt
4 cups powdered sugar
⅓ cup boiling water
1 (1-ounce) square bittersweet chocolate, chopped

Preheat oven to 375°. Grease 2 baking sheets. In a medium bowl, cream together butter and sugar until smooth. Beat in eggs one at a time, stir in milk, vanilla and lemon extract. In a separate bowl, combine cake flour and all-purpose flour, baking powder and salt; gradually blend into the creamed mixture. Drop dough in rounded tablespoons 2 inches apart on prepared baking sheet. Bake until edges begin to brown, about 20 to 30 minutes. Cool completely. Place powdered sugar in a large bowl. Mix boiling water 1 table-spoon at a time until the mixture is thick and spreadable. Set ½ of powdered sugar frosting aside. Place other half of frosting in double-boiler and stir in chocolate. Warm over low heat, stirring frequently, until chocolate melts. Remove from heat. With a brush, coat half of each cookie with chocolate frosting and the other half with white frosting. Set on waxed paper until frosting hardens.

Bloomington Convention and Visitors Bureau

Vermont Maple Pecan Cookies

3 cups old-fashioned oats
1 cup shredded unsweetened coconut
2⅔ cups flour
1 teaspoon salt
1 teaspoon cinnamon
2 cups packed light brown sugar
1 cup unsalted butter
½ cup maple syrup
2 tablespoons light corn syrup
2 teaspoons baking soda
¼ cup boiling water
1 teaspoon vanilla extract
2 cups chopped toasted pecans

Preheat oven to 300°. Position racks in the upper and lower thirds of the oven. Line two baking sheets with parchment paper. Combine oats, coconut, flour, salt, cinnamon and brown sugar in a large bowl; whisk to blend. Combine butter, maple syrup and corn syrup in a medium saucepan. Heat over medium heat until butter melts, stirring occasionally; remove from heat. In separate bowl, combine baking soda and boiling water, stirring to dissolve. Add to maple syrup mixture, stirring well. Add vanilla extract. Stir into dry ingredients. Add pecans; stir well. Place ¼-cup-size balls of dough on baking sheets, 3 inches apart. Flatten slightly. Bake 18 to 20 minutes, until golden brown and set, rotating positions halfway through baking. Cool on baking sheets 5 minutes; transfer to wire rack to cool completely. Makes 2½ dozen cookies.

Agate Days Celebration

Monster Cookies

1 cup sugar

1 cup brown sugar

½ cup butter, softened

¾ teaspoon vanilla

1¼ cups peanut butter

3 eggs

2 teaspoons baking soda

2½ cups quick oats

2½ cups flour

½ cup mini M & M's

½ cup chocolate chips

Preheat oven to 350°. Cream together sugars, butter, vanilla, peanut butter, eggs and baking soda. Add remaining ingredients. Batter will be very thick. Bake 8 to 10 minutes.

R&M Amish Tours

Sinclair Lewis' Sinful Christmas Cookies

Sinclair Lewis was very fond of cookies. He concocted this recipe in 1919. The cookies are rather addictive – one keeps coming back to the cookie jar for more.

2 sticks butter

2 cups sugar

1½ cups bread flour

5 tablespoons Nestle's cocoa

1 teaspoon salt

2 teaspoons almond extract

1 shot bourbon

2 eggs

½ cups sliced almonds

Preheat oven to 325°. In mixing bowl, cream together butter, sugar, flour, cocoa and salt. Add almond extract, bourbon and eggs, beating well. Mix in almonds by hand. Drop by heaping teaspoons on greased cookie sheets and bake 8 to 10 minutes, or until the cookies are firm on top. They should not brown around edges. Allow cookies to set 5 minutes. With metal spatula, transfer to wax paper-lined rack to cool. Store in air tight cookie jar or metal tin.

Sinclair Lewis - Sauk Centre

Pembroke Bakery's Favorite Chocolate Krinkles

½ cup butter
4 squares unsweetened
    chocolate
2 cups sugar
4 large eggs

2 cups flour
2 teaspoons baking soda
½ teaspoon salt
2 teaspoons vanilla

Melt butter and chocolate. Add sugar, bit by bit, until completely dissolved. Beat in eggs one at a time. Add remaining ingredients. Chill overnight. Shape and roll in powdered sugar.

Minnesota Boutiques

Biking in Sauk Centre

Pepparkakor (Spice or Gingersnaps)

1½ cups butter or margarine
1½ cups brown sugar
1 egg, beaten
1 teaspoon baking soda
4 tablespoons molasses
1 teaspoon ground cloves
1 teaspoon ground cinnamon
½ teaspoon ground ginger
3 cups flour

Combine butter, brown sugar, egg, baking soda and molasses; mix well and set aside. In separate bowl, combine cloves, cinnamon, ginger and flour. Combine 2 mixtures and refrigerate overnight. Roll out, not too thin, with different cutouts. Flour rolling pin and board to keep dough from sticking. Keep dough cold. Place on cookie sheet and bake at 400° for 8 to 10 minutes.

Carl Boberg
Santa Lucia Festival

Baklava

1 pound walnuts, chopped
1 teaspoon ground cinnamon

16 ounces phyllo dough
1 cup butter

Preheat oven to 350°. Toss nuts with cinnamon; set aside. Unroll phyllo dough, cover with damp cloth. Line bottom of 9x13-inch baking dish with 2 sheets of dough. Butter top of dough, and top with 2 more sheets. Repeat layers, buttering every second sheet, until 6 to 8 sheets thick. Top sheet should be buttered. Sprinkle 2 to 3 tablespoons nut mixture over dough. Cover with 6 to 8 sheets, buttering each 2nd sheet as done before. Cut into squares. Bake 50 minutes.

Sauce:

1 cup sugar
1 cup water

1 teaspoon vanilla extract
½ cup honey

Boil sugar and water until sugar is dissolved. Add vanilla and honey, simmer 20 minutes. Spoon sauce over warm baklava. Cool before serving. If left uncovered baklava will become soggy.

Greek Festival

Greek Festival

Last weekend in August

Saints Anargyroi Greek Orthodox Church
703 West Center Street • Rochester
507-282-1529
www.greekfestrochester.com

Rochester GreekFest began when a group of parishioners gathered together for a picnic with traditional food and dances. 50 years later it is a 3-day event and the longest running festival in the Rochester area.

Each August it gives visitors a chance to be "Greek for a day" because being Greek is as much a state of mind as it is a nationality, meaning to enjoy life to the fullest. The festival offers authentic Greek food, locally baked Greek pastries, live folk music, colorful Greek dancers, children games, marketplace, silent auction and a chance to tour the Church to see its unique architecture.

Admission and parking are always free and it is fully accessible. The most popular item is their famous baklava, still baked the traditional way.

Oatmeal Cookies

1 cup butter, softened
¾ cup brown sugar
¾ cup white sugar
2 eggs
2 cups flour
1 teaspoon salt

1 teaspoon baking soda
1 teaspoon vanilla
1 cup chocolate chips
3 cups quick oats
1 cup raisins

Preheat oven to 375°. Cream together butter, brown sugar and white sugar. Add eggs. Sift together flour, salt and baking soda; add to mixture. Add vanilla, chocolate chips, oats and raisins. Drop by rounded spoonfuls onto baking sheet. Bake 12 minutes.

Culturfest

Weird Laws

- Watch out, you can get arrested for teasing skunks. Don't call them Stinky!

- Please take that duck off the top of your head when crossing the state line, that sort of thing is illegal.

- If you're a man and you're driving a motorcycle, you must have on a shirt.

- Own a red car? Live in Minneapolis? You may not drive it down Lake Street.

- If you're in the mood for a hamburger, stay away from St. Cloud on Sundays when it is illegal to eat them.

Chocolate Bread Pudding

Pudding Mix:

4 cups heavy whipping cream
2 cups chocolate chips
2 cups white sugar
¾ cups brown sugar

2 cups eggs
2 tablespoons vanilla
1 gallon bread cubes*

*I use leftover breads. Buttermilk biscuits work great, as do sweet rolls (caramel, cinnamon, donuts, etc.).

In a saucepan over medium-low heat, heat cream; add chocolate chips to melt. Add sugars, eggs and vanilla; stir. Add cubed bread and mix, using hands. Place in 10x12-inch pan and bake at 325° for 1 hour and 15 minutes.

Kahlúa Sauce:

1 cup white sugar
2 cups cream (can use half-n-half or
    heavy cream)

½ cup Kahlúa
Corn starch for thickening

Mix sugar, cream and Kahlúa in heavy saucepan and bring to slow boil. Thicken with mixture of corn starch and water. Drizzle Kahlúa Sauce over WARM pudding. Can also drizzle hot fudge over top and add whipped cream.

Curtis Maas, Chef, The Cove
Wadena

Wadena

218-632-7704 • 877-631-7704
www.wadenachamber.com

Located at the cross roads of Highways 10, 71 and 29 in Central Minnesota, this downtown area offers experiences only a small town can. Take time to stroll the streets and alleyways and receive a thousand year Minnesota history lesson through 50 Alley Arts Murals on 18 buildings, each telling stories of Ojibwa life, mining, trapping, farming, the railroad and more. No longer in operation, the historic depot houses railroad history and the hands of time continue to run at Wadena County Historical Society Museum & Genealogy Research Center. Sports enthusiasts will really enjoy Wadena. There are trails for family and mountain biking, snowmobiling, kick sledding and cross country skiing. Swing away on the 18 hole public golf course. Sunnybrook Park and Campground is one of 13 parks in the community. It truly is a fantastic place.

Cold Yogurt Pumpkin Pudding

This is super easy. Impress your friends with this light, cold pudding.

1 cup plain regular or Greek yogurt
2 teaspoons pumpkin butter
1 tablespoon chopped walnuts
Dash cinnamon

Combine yogurt and pumpkin butter, mixing well. Garnish
with walnuts and cinnamon.

Center Creek Orchard

Pumpkin Fluff

1 (15-ounce) can pumpkin
10 ounces Cool Whip
1 package vanilla pudding
1 teaspoon pumpkin pie spice

Mix all ingredients, chill. Serve with graham crackers.

Center Creek Orchard

Chocolate Mousse

8 ounces bitter chocolate
8 ounces semi-sweet chocolate
½ cup Gran Marnier
1 pint heaving whipping cream
1 cup powdered sugar, sifted

Combine both chocolates and Gran Marnier in double-boiler; melt until smooth. Cool. In a separate bowl, beat whipping cream and powdered sugar together until smooth. Fold in chocolate mixture. Serve topped with whipped cream.

Tall Timber Days

Tall Timber Days

August

Tall Timber days is a celebration that has been happening in Grand Rapids for 32 years. The celebration was founded in order to honor the Logging Industry in the Itasca County area. This weekend long event kicks off on Friday with a street dance, complete with live music. A 5K race begins the festivities early on Saturday, and the weekend rounds out with delicious food, bingo, chainsaw carving demonstrations, arts and crafts, lumberjack shows, parades, turtle races and talent show. Of course, there is constant live music throughout the weekend. The center of the festival is the Education Tent, where visitors have a terrific opportunity to explore the history of the Northland, attend Sunday service and obtain general information.

Apple Dumplings

2 Granny Smith apples, peeled
   and cored
2 (8-ounce) tubes crescent rolls
1 cup butter
1½ cups sugar

1 teaspoon vanilla
Cinnamon to taste
1 (12-ounce) can Mountain Dew
Ice cream for serving

Preheat oven to 350°. Grease 9x13-inch baking dish. Cut each apple into 8 wedges and set aside. Separate crescent roll dough into triangles. Roll each apple wedge into crescent roll dough, starting with smallest end. Pinch to seal and place in baking dish. Melt butter in small saucepan and stir in sugar, vanilla and cinnamon. Pour butter mixture and Mountain Dew over dumplings. Bake 40 minutes or until golden brown. Spoon sauce from pan over each dumpling and serve with ice cream.

Center Creek Orchard

Hay Maze at Center Creek Orchard

Apple Pizza

Crust:
2⅓ to 3 cups flour, divided
3 tablespoons sugar
1 package active dry yeast
½ teaspoon salt

½ cup water
¼ cup milk
¼ cup butter, cubed

In large mixing bowl, combine 1½ cups flour, sugar, yeast and salt. In saucepan, heat water, milk and butter to 120° to 130°. Add to dry ingredients. Beat 2 minutes. Stir in remaining flour to form firm dough. Turn onto floured surface, cover and let rest 15 minutes.

Cream Cheese Filling:
12 ounces cream cheese, softened
¼ cup packed brown sugar

2 tablespoons caramel ice cream
   topping

In small mixing bowl, combine cream cheese, brown sugar and caramel.

Apple Filling:
4 cups sliced, peeled tart apples
2 tablespoons butter
½ cup sugar

2 tablespoons flour
1 teaspoon cinnamon

In large skillet, cook and stir apples in butter over medium heat 2 minutes. In a separate bowl, combine sugar, flour and cinnamon. Stir in skillet. Cook 3 minutes more. Reduce heat to low, cook uncovered, 4 to 6 minutes or until apples are tender, stirring frequently.

Oatmeal Topping:
⅓ cup quick oats
⅓ cup flour

⅓ cup sugar
¼ cup cold butter

Combine oatmeal, flour and sugar; cut in butter until crumbly.

Pat Crust dough onto a greased 14-inch pizza pan, building up edges slightly. Spread with Cream Cheese Filling, then Apple Filling. Sprinkle with Oatmeal Topping. Bake at 375° for 20 to 25 minutes or until crust is golden brown. Serve warm or cold.

Mattie Miller
Bluffscape Amish Tours

Polar Pete's Baked Alaska

1½ quarts Neapolitan ice cream, softened
9x5-inch piece of chiffon cake
1 cup sugar
½ cup light corn syrup
¼ cup water
4 ounces pasteurized egg whites, room temperature
½ teaspoon vanilla extract
Pinch kosher salt

Line 9x5-inch loaf pan with plastic wrap. Place ice cream into loaf pan and spread evenly. Place cake on top of ice cream, pressing down lightly. Place pan in freezer 1 hour. After 1 hour, combine sugar, corn syrup and water in a 2-quart saucepan and place over high heat. Stir just until sugar dissolves, about 5 minutes. With candy thermometer bring mixture to 240°.

While syrup is cooking, place egg whites, vanilla and salt into bowl of stand mixer and, using whisk attachment, whisk eggs on high speed until they reach medium peaks, 4 to 5 minutes.

When sugar syrup reaches 240°, remove from heat and, with stand mixer on low speed, slowly and carefully pour syrup in a thin, steady stream into egg white mixture, being careful not to come in contact with the whisk. Once all syrup has been added, increase mixer speed to high and whisk until stiff peaks are formed and mixture has cooled, 8 to 10 minutes.

Remove loaf pan from freezer, turn upside down onto a heatproof serving platter, and remove plastic wrap. Completely cover ice cream cake combo with 1-inch layer of meringue all around, sealing meringue to the pan around bottom edge. Use a propane torch to brown meringue all over. Serve immediately. May be frozen once meringue has browned.

Detroit Lakes Polar Fest

Grandma's Baked Alaska

1⅓ cups graham cracker crumbs, divided
¼ cup plus 6 tablespoons sugar, divided
¼ cup butter, softened
4 cups vanilla ice cream
3 egg whites
¼ teaspoon salt
1 teaspoon almond extract

Preheat oven to 375°. Set aside 3 tablespoons cracker crumbs for topping. Mix remaining cracker crumbs, ¼ cup sugar and butter together; press into 1 (9-inch) pie plate. Bake at 375° for 10 minutes. Place crust in freezer to cool and lay ice cream on counter to soften. When ice cream is softened, fill crust and freeze at least 1 hour or until ready to serve.

When ready to serve, preheat broiler to 500°. Beat egg whites till frothy. Add salt and almond extract; slowly add 6 tablespoons sugar, beating till stiff and glossy. Remove pie from freezer and top with meringue, sealing edges. Sprinkle with remaining crumbs. Place under broiler 2 minutes. Serve immediately.

Appeldoorn's Sunset Bay Resort

Gibbs Museum, St. Paul

Nano Ice Cream

Important! This recipe should be used in a controlled lab for science experiments only. Please keep in mind that liquid nitrogen is dangerous. It is 77° Kelvin. That is about 200° below zero Celsius or about 320° below zero Fahrenheit. Children should have adults present. Do not wear open toed shoes; wear goggles and heavy gloves. Also, make sure to close the liquid nitrogen container promptly.

Now, for the experiment!

If you were to make homemade ice cream you would use ice and salt to cool the liquid. Salt lowers the freezing point of water about 5 or 10 degrees Celsius. This process nucleates the grains inside the liquid but it usually takes about an hour worth of stirring to finish it. This recipe will use an alternate method and cool this liquid down really, really fast. Instead of ice and salt, it will be cooled using liquid nitrogen.

1 quart half-and-half	**8 tablespoons vanilla**
1 pint heavy cream	**1 liter liquid nitrogen**
1 cup sugar	**Metal mixing bowl**

Pour half-and-half, cream, sugar and vanilla into metal mixing bowl. Pour ½ of liquid nitrogen into bowl with cream mixture, stir gently. Continue to pour in liquid nitrogen and stir until smooth and cold.

Instead of taking an hour to make ice cream with ice and salt it is made it in a matter of seconds by cooling it really fast, resulting in tiny nucleated crystals or in other words, very, very smooth ice cream.

Science Museum of Minnesota

Science Museum of Minnesota

120 West Kellogg Boulevard • St. Paul
651-221-9444 • www.smm.org

Located on the banks of the Mississippi River in downtown St. Paul, the Science Museum of Minnesota has a 100+-year history of unforgettable science fun and learning.

With more than eight acres of indoor space devoted to hands-on exhibits and fascinating multimedia presentations, as well as an outdoor science park with activities focused on river ecology and landscape dynamics, exploring is the order of the day when visiting this fantastic museum. Enjoy a giant screen film in the state-of-the-art, convertible-dome Omnitheater, discover a world-class collection of fossils, touch a tornado, see an authentic Egyptian mummy, examine your cheek cells under a microscope, climb aboard a Mississippi River towboat, explore artifacts that span billions of years of the earth's history, play science-themed mini-golf, and much, much more.

Yukon Yummies

Ice Cream:

1 cup sugar
¼ teaspoon salt
7 egg yolks

1½ cups half-and-half
1 cup heavy cream
1 tablespoon vanilla extract

In a large mixing bowl, beat sugar, salt and egg yolks until thick and pale yellow; set aside. Bring half-and-half to simmer in medium saucepan. Do not allow it to boil over. Once half-and-half is hot, slowly beat hot half-and-half into egg mixture in a steady stream. The half-and-half should not be so hot that it scrambles the eggs. Pour entire mixture back into saucepan. Stir constantly with a whisk over medium-low heat until custard forms that will coat the back of a spoon. Remove from heat and pour hot custard through a strainer into a large, clean bowl. Allow custard to cool slightly. Stir in heavy cream and vanilla. Cover and refrigerate overnight. Stir chilled custard and freeze in 1 or 2 batches in an ice cream maker, following manufacturer's instructions. Transfer ice cream to small rectangular pan and freeze at least 2 hours. Place 2 dinner plates covered with waxed paper in freezer to chill. Using knife or cookie cutter, cut ice cream into 2-inch squares. Carefully place squares onto 1 chilled plate. Freeze overnight.

Candy Shell:

14 ounces bittersweet chocolate chips
4 tablespoons extra virgin coconut oil

Place chocolate chips in microwave-safe bowl and microwave until nearly all have melted, about 1 to 2 minutes. Stir in coconut oil and set aside. Mixture can be placed in refrigerator to cool, but keep checking, ensuring it does not completely cool. Work quickly when dipping ice cream into candy shell. Using a toothpick, quickly dip each square of ice cream into chocolate and place on second wax-covered chilled plate. Put treats into freezer to set 1 hour before serving. Makes about 20 bars.

Detroit Lake Polar Fest

Chocolate Port Cheesecake Tortes

Crust:

1 cup butter, melted
3¾ cups graham cracker crumbs

¾ cup sugar

Preheat oven to 350° with a water bath on the lowest rack. Combine butter, graham cracker crumbs, and sugar until moist throughout. Spread in a thin layer on bottom and up sides of 20 (5-inch) torte pans. Bake crusts 3 to 5 minutes.

Filling:

3 (8-ounce) packages cream cheese, softened
1 (14-ounce) can sweetened condensed milk
2 cups dark chocolate chips, melted

4 large eggs
2 teaspoons vanilla extract
300 ml Frontenac Desert Wine from Parley Lake Winery

In large mixing bowl, beat cream cheese until fluffy. Slowly add sweetened condensed milk and beat until smooth. Add remaining ingredients, mix well. Add ½ cup filling to each crust and bake 12 minutes or until center is set. Cool to room temperature and then chill. Serve with a drizzle of raspberry chipotle sauce. Makes 20 (5-inch) tortes.

Parley Lake Winery

Parley Lake Winery

8350 Parley Lake Road • Waconia
952-442-2290 • www.parleylakewinery.com

Experience the fine wine, rolling countryside and peaceful waters of Parley Lake Winery. They are located 'on the edge of the cities, out in the country' less than 10 minutes from the University of Minnesota Landscape Arboretum. The Winery prides itself on quality, food friendly wine, with more than 40 medals in National wine competitions including 8 Gold. Experience their tasting room located in a 130 year old Barn with tasting room professionals who provide an amazing wine experience, including a friendly education on the revolution in Cold Climate wines. The Winery gives detailed focus to the new University of Minnesota varietals including Marquette and La Crescent. Tours of the vineyard, winery and orchard are all part of what makes Parley Lake Winery a family friendly, wine educational experience. There are also many art and music events throughout the year so check their website for the latest details.

Gooey Chex Mix

1 (14-ounce) box Corn Chex Cereal
1 (7-ounce) bag sweetened coconut
1 (5-ounce) bag sliced almonds
1½ cups sugar
¾ cup butter
1¼ cups light corn syrup
Dash salt

Spray a large (the biggest you can find) bowl with non-stick cooking spray. Pour entire box of cereal, coconut and almonds. Gently mix together. In medium saucepan, combine sugar, butter, corn syrup and salt and cook over high heat. Bring to full boil, reduce heat to medium and cook 3 minutes, stirring constantly. Pour over cereal mixture; stir evenly. Spread cereal evenly on wax paper and cool completely. Break into pieces and store in air-tight container or zip-lock bag.

Mary Ebeling
Trimont FunFest

Trimont FunFest

Second Saturday in July

Anderson Memorial Park
www.TrimontFunFest.com
www.facebook.com/TrimontFunFest

Trimont FunFest is the annual summer celebration for the community of Trimont. Trimont is located on Highway 4, just 7 miles north of Interstate 90. Typical events include a medallion hunt, sand volleyball tournament, 3-on-3 basketball tournament, walk/run, BINGO, games, parade, hourly raffles, food, tractor / car / motorcycle show, silent auction, and all-day entertainment showcasing local talent. Other activities have included a float contest, pedal tractor pull, community church service, and carnival (complete with rides, games, bouncy houses, and food). FunFest is organized by a team of volunteers who are always looking for ways to keep FunFest fresh and lively while respecting the traditional family values of a small town.

Winter at Saint Croix Vineyards

White Christmas Mix

Minnesota winters are so cold, we often just put this outside on the deck to harden!

1 (17.5-ounce) box Crispix cereal
1 (14-ounce) box Frosted Cheerios
1 (12- to 14-ounce) bag Holiday M & M's
1 (12- to 14-ounce) bag Holiday Peanut M & M's
1 (10- to 12-ounce) bag pretzels
4 pounds white chocolate almond bark, melted

In large bowl, combine Crispix, Cheerios, regular and peanut M & M's and pretzels. Pour melted white chocolate over mix while stirring until all is coated. Spread onto several cookie sheets and place in freezer to harden. Break apart and store in containers.

Tracey Hays, owner
Bear Paw Resort

Bette LeMae

⅔ cup boiling water
1⅔ cups sugar
⅔ cup butter
3 ounces baker's bittersweet chocolate
1 cup semi-sweet chocolate chips
6 whole eggs

In saucepan, mix water and sugar; boil 2 minutes. Add butter, baker's chocolate and chocolate chips. Bring to a boil and boil 2 additional minutes. While mixture is boiling, beat eggs in mixing bowl. Slowly add boiled mixture to eggs, beating at low speed. Let mixture beat 2 to 3 minutes. Strain mixture into stainless steel bowl and pour into prepared wax-lined and floured 9-inch round pan. Place pan in hot water bath and bake 1 hour at 325°. When done, remove from water bath and place on towel. Scrape around side of pan and set 10 minutes.

Turn Bette LeMae over onto plate. Let cool 1 hour before frosting.

Frosting Glaze:

½ cup heavy whipping cream
1½ cups chocolate chips
Melted white chocolate

Scald whipping cream. Remove from heat and add chocolate chips; beat well. Let stand until cooled. Frost Bette LeMae and drizzle with melted white chocolate. Store in refrigerator.

Ruttger's Bay Lake Lodge

Cream Puff Dessert

½ cup butter
1 cup water
1 cup flour
4 eggs
2¾ cups milk

1 large package instant vanilla
   pudding mix
1 (8-ounce) package cream cheese,
   softened
1 cup whipping cream

Bring butter and water to a boil. Remove from heat and add flour, stir until ball forms and comes away from sides of pan. Add eggs, 1 at a time, beating after each addition. Pour mixture into lightly greased and floured 9x13-inch pan. Bake at 400° for 30 to 35 minutes. Remove from oven and set aside; cool. In separate bowl, mix milk and pudding; add cream cheese. Spread on cooled crust. Top with whipped cream. Drizzle with chocolate syrup or serve with fresh fruit.

Dorothy Bloemendaal, Murray County News
City of Slayton

The City of Slayton

has terrific events throughout the year.
Be sure to visit www.slaytonchamber.com
to learn details about when and
where to enjoy these celebrations.

Farm & Home Show

Chamber Annual Banquet

Shop Local Promotion

City Wide Rummage

Crazy Days

Prairie Day Parade

Pumpkin Fest

Tour of Homes

Holiday Open House

Kringle

Dough:

1 cup flour	1 tablespoon water
½ cup butter, softened	

Combine all ingredients and mix into soft, crumbly dough. Pat on cookie sheet in 2 long, 3-inch wide strips.

Filling:

1 cup water	3 eggs
½ cup butter	½ teaspoon real almond extract
1 cup flour	

Heat water and butter to boiling point. Remove from heat then add flour. Stir until smooth. Beat in 1 egg at a time, beating until smooth after each addition. Add almond extract. Spread lightly on Dough. Bake at 375° for 45 minutes.

Powdered Sugar Frosting:

1 cup powdered sugar	1 tablespoon cream
1 tablespoon butter (do not substitute)	1 teaspoon almond extract

Cream together all ingredients, mixing until light and creamy. Spread on cooled pastry. Toasted, sliced almonds can be sprinkled on top for garnish. At Christmas, sprinkle with red and green sugar crystals.

Sylvia Benson
Santa Lucia Festival

Berries from the Trail with Custard Sauce

1 cup raspberries
1 cup blueberries
8 egg yolks

½ cup sugar
1 cup marsala wine

Gently mix berries together and divide them among 4 serving dishes. Set aside. Bring 1-inch of water to simmer in medium saucepan. Whisk yolks and sugar together in bowl, preferably metal as it needs to be placed in saucepan. Set bowl of egg mixture in the pan of simmering (not boiling) water, and continue to whisk. As it cooks it will begin to thicken and turn pale yellow. When it begins to thicken, slowly whisk in wine. Continue to cook until very light and fluffy, about 4 to 5 minutes. Pour mixture over berries and serve immediately.

Lush Angel Dessert

1 prepared angel food cake (store bought is fine)
1 package instant vanilla pudding
1 (14-ounce) can sweetened condensed milk
1 cup water
1 (8-ounce) tub Cook Whip
1 teaspoon almond flavoring
Sliced strawberries and kiwi for garnish

Cut angel food cake into bite size pieces. Put ½ into 9x13-inch cake pan. Reserve the rest. Combine pudding mix, sweetened condensed milk and water together. Let stand until thickened. Fold in Cool Whip and almond flavoring. Put ½ pudding mixture on top of cake, then layer with reserved cake pieces. Pour remaining pudding mixture on top. Refrigerate no less than 4 hours. Garnish with sliced strawberries and kiwi.

Slayton Chamber of Commerce

Dessert Soup

2 cups prunes
1 cup raisins
1 cup sugar
1 stick cinnamon

½ cup tapioca
½ teaspoon salt
1 can cherry pie mix
1 large can frozen grape juice

Combine prunes, raisins, sugar and cinnamon in large pot. Cover with water and bring to a boil, stirring frequently until fruit is tender. Add tapioca and salt. When it starts to thicken, add cherry pie mix and grape juice. This makes a large amount. If it is too thick, add water.

Lois Berekvam
Stand Still Parade

Stand Still Parade

Rommegrot

1 stick butter
⅔ cup flour
1 pint half-and-half
1 pint whole milk
⅓ cup sugar

Melt butter in large pot over medium-high heat. Add flour
to make paste. Add half-and-half and milk. Bring to boil until thick while stirring constantly, being careful not to scorch.
Stir in sugar. Serve hot in small quantities. Delicious topped
with cinnamon and sugar.

Stand Still Parade

Stand Still Parade

3rd Saturday in May

Downtown Whalan
www.standstillparade.org

The parade began with the intention of
promoting community involvement and
just plain good old family fun. Since the
town is too small for a parade to move it
was decided the parade would stand still
and the spectators would do the moving.
The color guard and American Legion

members are always seated at the beginning of the parade, with all other units following. The
units are placed on each side of the street as well as down the center. Floats and units are
parked and musicians perform while standing in place. The parade stands still for one hour.
During the day there is live entertainment, food provided by the local church, and artists
demonstrating and selling art, children's activities and contests.

Maple Baked Oatmeal

6 cups milk
½ cup brown sugar
½ cup pure maple syrup
1½ tablespoons butter
1½ teaspoons cinnamon
¾ teaspoon nutmeg

1½ teaspoons vanilla
2 cups quick oats
1½ cups chopped apples
¾ cup Craisins
¾ cup slivered almonds

Preheat oven to 325° and lightly grease a 9x13-inch baking dish. Combine first 7 ingredients in large pan until butter is melted. Mix in remaining ingredients and spoon into greased baking dish. Bake 30 minutes.

Delicious topped with vanilla bean ice cream or whipped cream. We've often enjoyed it for breakfast!

Audubon Center of the North Woods

Index

Minnesota State Flower:
Pink and white lady's slipper
Cypripedium reginae

Index of Events & Destinations

This Index is meant to be a tool for locating all events and destinations featured in *Eat & Explore Minnesota*. Each event or destination is listed by both name and city referencing the page number for its featured page. Events and destinations that have a recipe are additionally listed by event or destination name then recipe, referencing the page number for the recipe. A complete Index of Recipes begins on page 255.

A

Agate Days Celebration 78
Almond Butter Crunch 202
Cheesy Bread 71
Crockpot Beef Stew 50
Kerin Fahland 160
Pecan Pie Mini Muffins 78
Vermont Maple Pecan Cookies 218

Albert Lea
Albert Lea Convention and Visitors
   Bureau 59
Big Island Rendezvous and Festival 162
Freeborn County Historical Museum,
   Library and Village 147

**Albert Lea Convention and Visitors
   Bureau 59**
Chicken Tetrazzini 133
Hot Corn Dip 10
Spinach Salad 59

Alexandria
Douglas County Fair 69
Just a Jaunt 131
Northland Woolens 130

A maze'n Farmyard 92
Apple Delight 206
Deluxe Hotdish 134
Garlic Roasted Asparagus 92
Pleasin' Popovers 72
Teriyaki Chicken Wings 127

**American Indian Learning Resource
   Center 215**

Amish Tours of Harmony 74
Buttermilk Pie 194
Corner Cake, A (Wedding Cake) 180
Honey Wheat Bread 74
Shoo-Fly Pie 196

Appeldoorn's Sunset Bay Resort 23
Appeldoorn's Beer Cheese Dip 11
Appeldoorn's Oyster Stew 46
Cheesy Potato Slices 99
Escalloped Corn (Squaw Corn) 106
Golden Beans Au Gratin 105
Grandma's Baked Alaska 231
Lemon Poppy Seed Bread 81
Pepperoni Pizza Pita Pockets 23
Ramen Noodle Salad 61

Snicker's Cake 180
Sweet-N-Sour Meatballs 143

Apple Festival 204

Audubon Center of the North Woods 209
Maple Apple Crisp 208
Maple Baked Oatmeal 244
Maple Glazed Sweet Potatoes with Bacon
  and Caramelized Onions 115
North Country Basting Sauce 176
Pumpkin Dessert 209
Stuffed Peppers 148

B

Bear Paw Resort 63
Bear Paw Resort's Rhubarb Crunch 201
Buckeye Brownies 216
Feta Cheese and Pistachio Spread 16
Minnes"O"ta Cucumber Salad 63
Tomato Basil Soup 40
White Christmas Mix 237

Beaver Bay
Cove Point Lodge 137

Bemidji
Santa Lucia Festival 84

Big Island Rendezvous and Festival 162
Bob Lauer's Father's Rib Recipe 159
Chocolate Cobbler 199
Grilled Fish 169
Orange Glazed Mini Muffins 77
Quinoa with Fish 170
Tasty Tilapia 162
Zesty Halibut 171

Black Lantern Resort and Retreat 17
Baby Corn Salad 65

Sally's Wild Rice Soup 37
Spicy Minnesota Spread 17
Tortellini Cranberry Salad 66

Bloomington 42
Bloomington Convention and Visitors
  Bureau 42

Bloomington Convention and Visitors Bureau
Black & White Cookies 217
Chicken Stir-Fry 126
Chili Cheese Dip 11
Crockpot Beer Cheese Soup 42
Crockpot Chili 51
Potato Pancakes 86
Taco Salad 60

Bluffscape Amish Tours 116
Apple Pizza 229
Apple-Walnut Salad 58
Bacon Wrapped Water Chestnuts 116
Tavern Burgers 146
Wild Rice Soup 36

Brainerd, Minnesota's Playground 188
Beer Batter 173
Country Sampler Picnic 189
Rhubarb Cake 188
Venison Stroganoff 161

Brooklyn Park
Farmers Market 96
Tater Daze 97

Burnsville 64
Bleu Cheese Dressing 64

Buttered Corn Days 111
Corn Bake 110
Corn Casserole 111
Corn Frittata 109

C

Center Creek Orchard 203
Apple Dumplings 228
Apple Oatmeal Crisp 203
Apple Pie Stuffed French Toast 85
Apple Pineapple Salad 68
Baked Apples 114
Cold Yogurt Pumpkin Pudding 226
No Crust Pumpkin Pie 197
Pumpkin Cream Cheese Pie 197
Pumpkin Fluff 226
Roasted Pumpkin Seeds 24
Chanhassen
Axels Charhouse 214
Chickadee Boutique 12
5 Minute Chocolate Cake in a Mug 182
Texas Salsa 12
Toasted Almond Party Spread 16
Chisholm
St. Louis County Fair 89
Country Sampler Picnic 189
Cove Point Lodge 137
Cove Point's Lucca Pasta 137
Culturfest 45
Apfelstrudel (Apple Strudel) 205
Banana Bread 80
Better-For-You Mac & Cheese 123
Brazilian Black Bean Soup 43
Broccoli Casserole 113
Chinese Brown Gravy 175
Chinese Coleslaw 62
Chinese Noodle Casserole 153
English Raisin Cake 181
French Potato Pancakes 86
Garden Patch Soup 45
He-Man's Stew 50
Hungarian Goulash 151
Italian Stuffed Peppers 149
Limpa 75
Meatloaf 141
Mexican Goulash 118
Norwegian Apple Pie 192
Oatmeal Cookies 224
O'Henry Bars 212
Scalloped Potatoes 99
Shrimp and Pea Rice Bowl 168
Split Pea Soup 44
Streusel Coffee Cake 179
Swedish Meatballs with Gravy 142
Tater Tot Hot Dish 94
Texas Hash 144
Thyme Mushroom Gravy 175
Zucchini Bread 80

D

Dakota Day 54
Deardorff Orchards and Vineyards 25
Blue Cashew Truffles 25
Fresh Apple Cake 191
Deerwood
Ruttger's Bay Lake Lodge 198
Delano
Woodland Hill Winery 101
Detroit Lakes
Detroit Lakes Polar Fest 56

Detroit Lakes Polar Fest 56
    Fresh Green Salad with Almonds &
        Craisins 57
    Grilled Bacon-Wrapped Waterfowl 138
    Hibernation Fry Bread 82
    Pete's Reindeer Stew 47
    Polar Pete's Baked Alaska 230
    Wild Rice and Edamame Salad 53
    Yukon Yummies 234
Douglas County Fair 69
    Carnival Popcorn Salad 69
    County Fair Chicken Bake 128
    Fish Pond Salmon Spread 21
    Roller Coaster Potato Salad 65
Duluth
    Beacon Pointe Resort 167
    Edgewater Hotel and Waterpark 184

E

Eden Valley
    A maze'n Farmyard 92
Edgewater Hotel and Waterpark 184
    Pound Cake for Choco-holics 184

F

Fairmont
    Fall Festival at Center Creek Orchard 203
Fall Festival at Center Creek Orchard 203
Farmers Market 96
Freeborn County Historical Museum,
    Library and Village 147
    Pat's Crumble Burgers 147

G

General Store of Minnetonka 52
    General Store Café Wild Rice Apple Salad 52
    Oatmeal Carmelitas 210
Gibbs Museum of Pioneer and Dakota Life 83
    Apple Crisp for a Crowd 204
    Christmas Stewed Fruit 67
    Dakota Day Wild Rice Salad 54
    Soul Cakes 83
Glenwood 139
    International Hetteen Vintage Snowmobile
        Races 139
    Kids Day 139
    Magical Christmas in Glenwood 139
    Pope County Community Expo 139
    Pope County Free Fair 139
    Pope County Fright Nights 139
    Waterama 139
    Winterama 139
Glenwood Chamber of Commerce
    Chilly Day Wild Rice Soup 36
    Pheasant Meatloaf 138
    Spring Salad 55
    Taco Party Dip 13
Grand Marais
    East Bay Suites 167
Grand Rapids
    Tall Timber Days 227
Greek Festival 223
    Baklava 223

H

Hackensack
    Hyde-A-Way Bay Resort 155

Harmony
Amish Tours of Harmony 74
Slim's Woodshed 129
Hyde-A-Way Bay Resort 155
Bean Dip 14
Beef Burrito Skillet 144
French Dip 155
Lemon Shrimp 169
Peanut Butter Fingers 213
Piña Colada Fruit Salad 68
Popovers 72
Pumpkin Pancakes 87
Slow Cooker Chicken in Mushroom
Gravy 131

I

Isle
Appeldoorn's Sunset Bay Resort 23

J

Just a Jaunt 131

L

Lanesboro
Bluffscape Amish Tours 116
R&M Amish Tours 219
Little Falls
Little Falls Convention and Visitors
Bureau 187
**Little Falls Convention and Visitors
Bureau 187**
Chicken and Bacon Roll-Ups 135
Miniature Blueberry Cheesecakes 187
"Real" Mac & Cheese 122

Loretto
Axels Charhouse 214
Lutsen
Caribou Highlands Lodge 166, 167
Moguls Grille and Tap Room at Caribou
Highlands Lodge 166

M

Madelia
Younger Brothers Capture 104
Mankato
Ribfest 112
Mendota
Axels Charhouse 214
Minneapolis
Minneapolis Greek Festival 18
Polish American Cultural Institute of
Minnesota 152
Taste Twin Cities Food & Drink Tours 178
Twin Cities Polish Festival 49
Minneapolis Greek Festival 18
Hummus 18
Minnesota Boutiques 70
Janet Bennett's Bumstead's 70
Pembroke Bakery's Favorite Chocolate
Krinkles 221
Minnetonka
General Store of Minnetonka 52
Moose Lake
Agate Days Celebration 78
First National Bank of Moose Lake 78
Muskie Days Music Festival 28
Hot Island Russian Lullaby Tea 28

N

Nevis 29
  Muskie Days Music Festival 28
New Brighton
  Stockyard Days 41
Nickle Dickle Day 207
  Deardorff Apple Crisp 207
Northern Rail Traincar Inn 145
Northland Woolens 130
  Chicken Hotdish 130
  Coffee Creamer 33

O

Odyssey Resorts 166, 167
  Bourbon Planked Salmon 167
  S'mores Brownie Cake 183
Owatonna
  Culturfest 45

P

Park Rapids
  Bear Paw Resort 63
Parley Lake Winery 235
  Asparagus, Mushroom and Gorgonzola
    Risotto 93
  Chocolate Port Cheesecake Tortes 235
Pequot Lakes
  Towering Pines Resort 38
Pioneer Christmas 67
Pleasant Valley Orchard 158
  Easy Strawberry Cake 189
  Pork Chops and Apples 158
  Sweet Potato Apple Casserole 114
**Polish American Cultural Institute of
    Minnesota 152**

Preston 20
  Chicken Crêpes 132
  Smoked Trout Paté 20

R

R&M Amish Tours 219
  Delicious Barbecued Meatballs 142
  Monster Cookies 219
  Peanut Butter Squares 213
RibFest 112
  Broccoli Corn Casserole 112
Rochester
  Greek Festival 223
Roseville
  Axels Charhouse 214
  Roseville Visitors Association 215
Roseville Visitors Association 215
  Axel's Spicy Penne 136
  Blackened Swordfish 172
  Key's Café All American Apple Pie 193
  Wild Rice Krispy Bars 215
Ruttger's Bay Lake Lodge 198
  Bette LeMae 238
  Butterfinger Cream Pie 198
  Cabbage Soup 39
  Corn Muffins 79
  Pork Medallions with Mango 157
  Potato-Crusted Walleye with Cucumber
    Sour Cream Dressing 164
  Wild Rice & Toasted Almond Pilaf 119
  Zig's Hot Artichoke Dip 15

S

St. Cloud
  Stearns History Museum 150

Saint Croix Vineyards 31
   Raspberry Infusion Cocktail 31
St. Louis County Fair 89
   Walnut Chicken Spread 19
   Lefse 89
St. Paul
   Apple Festival 204
   Dakota Day 54
   Gibbs Museum of Pioneer and Dakota
     Life 83
   Pioneer Christmas 67
   Science Museum of Minnesota 233
   Wabasha Street Caves 73
Sandstone
   Audubon Center of the North Woods 209
   The Syruping Day 208
Santa Lucia Festival 84
   Kringle 240
   Pepparkakor (Spice or Gingersnaps) 222
   Swedish Almond Toast 84
   Swedish Bacon Pancake 88
Sauk Centre 220
   Sinclair Lewis' Sinful Christmas
     Cookies 220
Science Museum of Minnesota 233
   Nano Ice Cream 232
Sever's Corn Maze and Fall Festival 108
   Country Corn Casserole 108
Shafer
   Pleasant Valley Orchard 158
Shakopee
   Sever's Corn Maze and Fall Festival 108
   Taste of Shakopee 107

Shevlin
   Black Lantern Resort and Retreat 17
Shoreview
   Chickadee Boutique 12
Slayton
   Cream Puff Dessert 239
   Left Bank Café, The 200
   Murray County News 239
   Rhubarb Crunch 200
   Slayton Chamber of Commerce 200
Slayton Chamber of Commerce 200, 239
   Cheesy Broccoli and Chicken Casserole 135
   Country-Style Pork Ribs 160
   Do-Ahead Garlic Mashed Potatoes 100
   Granny's Applesauce Meatloaf 141
   Honey-Mustard Glazed Carrots 102
   Lush Angel Dessert 241
Sleepy Eye 110
   Buttered Corn Days 111
Slim's Woodshed 129
Sonshine Music Festival 174
Spirit Lake Steakhouse 98
   Minotte's Steak Sinatra 154
   Rosemary Roman Potatoes 98
Stand Still Parade 243
   Artichoke Dip 15
   Basic Pie Crust 194
   Black Bottom Cupcakes 186
   Bucky's Lefse 90
   Cheese-Scalloped Carrots 103
   Cream Cheese Frosting 185
   Dessert Soup 242
   Fresh Guacamole 13
   Hamburger Pie 151

Italian Zucchini Pie 117
Oriental Chicken Wings 26
Rommegrot 243
Salmon Party Log 21
Sloppy Joes 146
Slow Cooker Stuffing 120
Spaghetti with Fresh Vegetables Sauce 121

Stearns History Museum 150
Polish Hotdish 150

Stillwater
Saint Croix Vineyards 31

Stockyard Days 41
Broccoli Cheese Soup 41
Easy Chow Mein 153
Tantalizing Tilapia 163

Syruping Day, The 208

T

Tall Timber Days 227
Coolers 30
Chocolate Mousse 227
Marinade 176

Taste of Shakopee 107
Jumbo Shells 140
Salmon Sandwich Bake 166
Tomato and Corn Scallop 107

Taste Twin Cities Food & Drink Tours 178
Cinnamon Roll Cake 178

Tater Daze 97
Baked Breakfast Hash Browns 95
Hockey Skins 26
Max's Potatoes 96
Potatoes with Leeks 97

Towering Pines Resort 38
Minnesota Blueberry Muffins 76
Minnesota Vacation Chicken Wild Rice
Soup 38
Pistachio Ambrosia Salad 66

Trimont
Trimont FunFest 236

Trimont FunFest 236
Corn Fritters 109
Gooey Chex Mix 236
Kahlúa Bread 81
Snickerdoodle Bars 211
Special K Bars 214

Twin Cities Polish Festival 49
Cabbage Rolls (Golabki) 152
Chocolate Mazurek 185
Hunter's Stew 48

Two Harbors
Grand Superior Lodge 167
Larsmont Cottages 167
Ledge Rock Grille at Larsmont Cottages 166
Northern Rail Traincar Inn 145
Splashing Rock Restaurant at Grand Superior
Lodge 166

W

Wabasha
Minnesota Boutiques 70

Wabasha Street Caves 73
Baking Powder Biscuits 73
Beef and Pork Roast 156
Ham and Dill Pickle Appetizer Bites 22
Strawberry Short Cake 190
Taco Salad 60

Waconia
    Deardorff Orchards and Vineyards 25
    Nickle Dickle Day 207
    Parley Lake Winery 235

Wadena
    Wadena Chamber of Commerce 225

Wadena Chamber of Commerce 225
    Chicken Hotties 128
    Chocolate Bread Pudding 225
    Easter Pizza 124
    Marinated Chicken Wings 127

Wahkon
    Spirit Lake Steakhouse 98

Walker
    Beachfire Bar and Grille at Trapper's
        Landing Lodge 166
    Trapper's Landing Lodge 167

Whalan
    Stand Still Parade 243

Winona
    Apple-Romaine Salad 58
    Pecan Apple Pie 195
    Walleye Cakes 165

Winona – Historic Island City 195
Willmar
    Sonshine Music Festival 174

Woodbury
    Axels Charhouse 214

Woodland Hill Winery 101

Y

Younger Brothers Capture 104
    Calico Bean Bake 104
    Pickled Jalapeños 22
    Rhubarb Slush 29

Llamas at Northland Woolens

Index of Recipes

A

Almonds
    Almond Butter Crunch 202
    Chicken Hotdish 130
    Chinese Coleslaw 62
    Chinese Noodle Casserole 153
    Fresh Green Salad with Almonds & Craisins 57
    Kringle 240
    Lush Angel Dessert 241
    Maple Baked Oatmeal 244
    Ramen Noodle Salad 61
    Sinclair Lewis' Sinful Christmas Cookies 220
    Swedish Almond Toast 84
    Toasted Almond Party Spread 16
    Wild Rice and Edamame Salad 53
    Wild Rice & Toasted Almond Pilaf 119
Apfelstrudel (Apple Strudel) 205
Appeldoorn's Beer Cheese Dip 11
Appeldoorn's Oyster Stew 46
Appetizers. *See also* Dips
    Blue Cashew Truffles 25
    Feta Cheese and Pistachio Spread 16
    Fish Pond Salmon Spread 21
    Garlic-Cheese Spread 19
    Ham and Dill Pickle Appetizer Bites 22
    Hockey Skins 26
    Hummus 18
    Oriental Chicken Wings 26
    Party Sandwiches 27
    Pepperoni Pizza Pita Pockets 23
    Pickled Jalapeños 22
    Roasted Pumpkin Seeds 24
    Salmon Party Log 21
    Smoked Trout Paté 20
    Spicy Minnesota Spread 17

    Toasted Almond Party Spread 16
    Walnut Chicken Spread 19
Apples
    Apfelstrudel (Apple Strudel) 205
    Apple Crisp for a Crowd 204
    Apple Delight 206
    Apple Dumplings 228
    Apple Oatmeal Crisp 203
    Apple Pie Stuffed French Toast 85
    Apple Pineapple Salad 68
    Apple Pizza 229
    Apple-Romaine Salad 58
    Apple-Walnut Salad 58
    Baked Apples 114
    Deardorff Apple Crisp 207
    Fresh Apple Cake 191
    Fresh Green Salad with Almonds & Craisins 57
    General Store Café Wild Rice Apple Salad 52
    Granny's Applesauce Meatloaf 141
    Harvest Apple Pie 192
    Hunter's Stew 48
    Key's Café All American Apple Pie 193
    Maple Apple Crisp 208
    Maple Baked Oatmeal 244
    Norwegian Apple Pie 192
    Pecan Apple Pie 195
    Pork Chops and Apples 158
    Spring Salad 55
    Sweet Potato Apple Casserole 114
    Wassail 34
Artichoke
    Artichoke Dip 15
    Lemon Shrimp 169
    Stuffed Artichokes 113
    Zig's Hot Artichoke Dip 15

Asparagus
    Asparagus, Mushroom/Gorgonzola Risotto 93
    Chicken Crêpes 132
    Garlic Roasted Asparagus 92
Avocado, Fresh Guacamole 13
Axel's Spicy Penne 136

B

Baby Corn Salad 65
Bacon Wrapped Water Chestnuts 116
Baked Apples 114
Baked Breakfast Hash Browns 95
Baking Powder Biscuits 73
Baklava 223
Banana Bread 80
Banana Pancakes 87
Bar Cookies
    Buckeye Brownies 216
    Oatmeal Carmelitas 210
    O'Henry Bars 212
    Peanut Butter Fingers 213
    Peanut Butter Squares 213
    Snickerdoodle Bars 211
    Special K Bars 214
    Wild Rice Krispy Bars 215
Basic Pie Crust 194
Beans
    Baby Corn Salad 65
    Bean Dip 14
    Beef Burrito Skillet 144
    Brazilian Black Bean Soup 43
    Calico Bean Bake 104
    Chili Cheese Dip 11
    Crockpot Chili 51
    Golden Beans Au Gratin 105
    Hamburger Pie 151
    Hummus 18
    Kerin Fahland 160
    Mexican Goulash 118

    Taco Salad 60
    Tater Tot Hot Dish 94
    Texas Salsa 12
    White Chicken Chili 51
    Wild Rice and Edamame Salad 53
Béarnaise Sauce 172
Bear Paw Resort's Rhubarb Crunch 201
Beef. *See also* Chili, Meatballs, Meatloaf,
    Sausage, Stew
    Beef and Pork Roast 156
    Beef Burrito Skillet 144
    Beef Stroganoff 145
    Cabbage Rolls 152
    Calico Bean Bake 104
    Chili Cheese Dip 11
    Easy Chow Mein 153
    French Dip 155
    Garden Patch Soup 45
    Hamburger Pie 151
    Hungarian Goulash 151
    Italian Stuffed Peppers 149
    Jumbo Shells 140
    Minotte's Steak Sinatra 154
    Pat's Crumble Burgers 147
    Polish Hotdish 150
    Sloppy Joes 146
    Stuffed Peppers 148
    Taco Salad 60
    Tater Tot Hot Dish 94
    Tavern Burgers 146
    Texas Hash 144
Beer
    Appeldoorn's Beer Cheese Dip 11
    Beer Batter 173
    Crockpot Beer Cheese Soup 42
Berries from the Trail with Custard Sauce 241
Best-Ever Brown Gravy 174
Bette LeMae 238
Better-For-You Mac & Cheese 123

Beverages. *See also* Punch
    Coffee Creamer 33
    Coolers 30
    Hot Island Russian Lullaby Tea 28
    Mocha Cooler 34
    Raspberry Infusion Cocktail 31
    Rhubarb Slush 29
    Sweet and Spiced Coffee 33
    Wassail 34
Biscuits, Baking Powder 73
Black Bottom Cupcakes 186
Blackened Swordfish 172
Black & White Cookies 217
Bleu Cheese Dressing 64
Blueberry
    Berries from the Trail with Custard Sauce 241
    Dakota Day Wild Rice Salad 54
    Miniature Blueberry Cheesecakes 187
    Minnesota Blueberry Muffins 76
    Piña Colada Fruit Salad 68
Blue Cashew Truffles 25
Bob Lauer's Father's Rib Recipe 159
Bourbon Planked Salmon 167
Brazilian Black Bean Soup 43
Breads. *See also* Biscuits, Muffins, Pancakes
    Apple Dumplings 228
    Apple Pie Stuffed French Toast 85
    Banana Bread 80
    Bucky's Lefse 90
    Cheesy Bread 71
    Chocolate Bread Pudding 225
    Corn Fritters 109
    Hibernation Fry Bread 82
    Honey Wheat Bread 74
    Kahlúa Bread 81
    Lefse 89
    Lemon Poppy Seed Bread 81
    Limpa 75
    Pleasin' Popovers 72
    Popovers 72
    Slow Cooker Stuffing 120

    Soul Cakes 83
    Swedish Almond Toast 84
    Zucchini Bread 80
Broccoli
    Broccoli Casserole 113
    Broccoli Cheese Soup 41
    Broccoli Corn Casserole 112
    Cheesy Broccoli and Chicken Casserole 135
Buckeye Brownies 216
Bucky's Lefse 90
Burgers. *See* Sandwiches
Butterfinger Cream Pie 198
Buttermilk Pie 194

C

Cabbage
    Cabbage Rolls 152
    Cabbage Soup 39
    Chinese Coleslaw 62
    He-Man's Stew 50
    Hunter's Stew 48
    Minnes"O"ta Cucumber Salad 63
    Ramen Noodle Salad 61
    Taco Salad 60
Cakes
    Black Bottom Cupcakes 186
    Chocolate Mazurek 185
    Cinnamon Roll Cake 178
    Corner Cake, A (Wedding Cake) 180
    Easy Strawberry Cake 189
    English Raisin Cake 181
    5 Minute Chocolate Cake in a Mug 182
    Fresh Apple Cake 191
    Miniature Blueberry Cheesecakes 187
    Pound Cake for Choco-holics 184
    Rhubarb Cake 188
    S'mores Brownie Cake 183
    Snicker's Cake 180
    Strawberry Short Cake 190
    Streusel Coffee Cake 179

Calico Bean Bake 104
Caramel
　Apple Pizza 229
　Oatmeal Carmelitas 210
　Snicker's Cake 180
Carnival Popcorn Salad 69
Carrots
　Apple-Romaine Salad 58
　Beef and Pork Roast 156
　Brazilian Black Bean Soup 43
　Broccoli Cheese Soup 41
　Cheese-Scalloped Carrots 103
　Chinese Coleslaw 62
　Crockpot Beef Stew 50
　Garden Patch Soup 45
　He-Man's Stew 50
　Honey-Mustard Glazed Carrots 102
　Hunter's Stew 48
　Pete's Reindeer Stew 47
　Sally's Wild Rice Soup 37
　Split Pea Soup 44
　Stuffed Peppers 148
　Tomato Basil Soup 40
　Wild Rice and Edamame Salad 53
Cashew Truffles, Blue 25
Catfish, Grilled Fish 169
Cauliflower, Better-For-You Mac & Cheese 123
Champagne Punch 32
Cheesecakes, Miniature Blueberry 187
Cheesecake Tortes, Chocolate Port 235
Cheese-Scalloped Carrots 103
Cheesy Bread 71
Cheesy Broccoli and Chicken Casserole 135
Cheesy Potato Slices 99
Chicken
　Axel's Spicy Penne 136
　Cheesy Broccoli and Chicken Casserole 135
　Chicken and Bacon Roll-Ups 135
　Chicken Crêpes 132
　Chicken Hotdish 130

Chicken Hotties 128
Chicken Stir-Fry 126
Chicken Tetrazzini 133
County Fair Chicken Bake 128
Cove Point's Lucca Pasta 137
Deluxe Hotdish 134
Marinated Chicken Wings 127
Minnesota Vacation Chicken Wild Rice Soup 38
Oriental Chicken Wings 26
Rosemary and Garlic Roasted Chicken 129
Sally's Wild Rice Soup 37
Slow Cooker Chicken in Mushroom Gravy 131
Teriyaki Chicken Wings 127
Walnut Chicken Spread 19
White Chicken Chili 51
Chili Cheese Dip 11
Chili, Crockpot 51
Chili, White Chicken 51
Chilly Day Wild Rice Soup 36
Chinese Brown Gravy 175
Chinese Coleslaw 62
Chinese Noodle Casserole 153
Chocolate
　Almond Butter Crunch 202
　Bette LeMae 238
　Black Bottom Cupcakes 186
　Black & White Cookies 217
　Buckeye Brownies 216
　Butterfinger Cream Pie 198
　Chocolate Bread Pudding 225
　Chocolate Cobbler 199
　Chocolate Mazurek 185
　Chocolate Mousse 227
　Chocolate Port Cheesecake Tortes 235
　5 Minute Chocolate Cake in a Mug 182
　Kahlúa Bread 81
　Mocha Cooler 34
　Monster Cookies 219
　Oatmeal Carmelitas 210
　Oatmeal Cookies 224
　O'Henry Bars 212

Peanut Butter Fingers 213
Peanut Butter Squares 213
Pembroke Bakery's…Chocolate Krinkles 221
Pound Cake for Choco-holics 184
Sinclair Lewis' Sinful Christmas Cookies 220
S'mores Brownie Cake 183
Snicker's Cake 180
Special K Bars 214
White Christmas Mix 237
Yukon Yummies 234
Christmas Stewed Fruit 67
Cinnamon Roll Cake 178
Cobblers and Crisps
Almond Butter Crunch 202
Apple Crisp for a Crowd 204
Apple Oatmeal Crisp 203
Bear Paw Resort's Rhubarb Crunch 201
Chocolate Cobbler 199
Deardorff Apple Crisp 207
Maple Apple Crisp 208
Rhubarb Crunch 200
Coffee
Coffee Creamer 33
Mocha Cooler 34
Sweet and Spiced Coffee 33
Cold Yogurt Pumpkin Pudding 226
Coleslaw
Chinese Coleslaw 62
Ramen Noodle Salad 61
Taco Salad 60
Cookies. See also Bar Cookies
Black & White Cookies 217
Monster Cookies 219
Oatmeal Cookies 224
Pembroke Bakery's…Chocolate Krinkles 221
Pepparkakor (Spice or Gingersnaps) 222
Sinclair Lewis' Sinful Christmas Cookies 220
Vermont Maple Pecan Cookies 218
Coolers 30

Corn
Baby Corn Salad 65
Bean Dip 14
Broccoli Corn Casserole 112
Corn Bake 110
Corn Casserole 111
Corn Frittata 109
Corn Fritters 109
Corn Muffins 79
Country Corn Casserole 108
Escalloped Corn (Squaw Corn) 106
Hot Corn Dip 10
Mexican Goulash 118
Tater Tot Hot Dish 94
Texas Salsa 12
Tomato and Corn Scallop 107
Corner Cake, A (Wedding Cake) 180
Country Corn Casserole 108
Country-Style Pork Ribs 160
County Fair Chicken Bake 128
Cove Point's Lucca Pasta 137
Craisins
Dakota Day Wild Rice Salad 54
Fresh Green Salad with Almonds & Craisins 57
General Store Café Wild Rice Apple Salad 52
Maple Baked Oatmeal 244
Spring Salad 55
Wild Rice and Edamame Salad 53
Cranberry
Apple-Walnut Salad 58
County Fair Chicken Bake 128
Tortellini Cranberry Salad 66
Cream Cheese Frosting 185
Cream Puff Dessert 239
Crisps. See Cobblers and Crisps
Crockpot Beef Stew 50
Crockpot Beer Cheese Soup 42
Crockpot Chili 51
Crunch. See Cobblers and Crisps

Cucumber
  Minnes"O"ta Cucumber Salad 63
  Potato-Crusted Walleye with Cucumber Sour
    Cream Dressing 164
  Quinoa with Fish 170
Cupcakes, Black Bottom 186

D

Dakota Day Wild Rice Salad 54
Deardorff Apple Crisp 207
Delicious Barbecued Meatballs 142
Deluxe Hotdish 134
Desserts. *See also* Bar Cookies, Cakes, Cobblers and
    Crisps, Cookies, Puddings
  Almond Butter Crunch 202
  Apfelstrudel (Apple Strudel) 205
  Apple Delight 206
  Apple Dumplings 228
  Baklava 223
  Bear Paw Resort's Rhubarb Crunch 201
  Berries from the Trail with Custard Sauce 241
  Bette LeMae 238
  Chocolate Port Cheesecake Tortes 235
  Cream Puff Dessert 239
  Dessert Soup 242
  Gooey Chex Mix 236
  Kringle 240
  Lush Angel Dessert 241
  Pumpkin Dessert 209
  Pumpkin Fluff 226
  Rhubarb Crunch 200
  Rommegrot 243
  White Christmas Mix 237
Dips
  Appeldoorn's Beer Cheese Dip 11
  Artichoke Dip 15
  Bean Dip 14
  Chili Cheese Dip 11
  Fresh Guacamole 13
  Hot Corn Dip 10
  Taco Party Dip 13

Texas Salsa 12
Zig's Hot Artichoke Dip 15
Do-Ahead Garlic Mashed Potatoes 100
Dumplings 47
Dumplings, Apple 228

E

Easter Pizza 124
Easy Chow Mein 153
Easy Strawberry Cake 189
Edamame Salad, Wild Rice and 53
English Raisin Cake 181
Escalloped Corn (Squaw Corn) 106

F

Feta Cheese and Pistachio Spread 16
Fish. *See* specific fish
Fish Pond Salmon Spread 21
5 Minute Chocolate Cake in a Mug 182
French Dip 155
French Potato Pancakes 86
French Toast, Apple Pie Stuffed 85
Fresh Apple Cake 191
Fresh Green Salad with Almonds & Craisins 57
Fresh Guacamole 13
Frittata, Corn 109
Fritters, Corn 109
Frosting, Cream Cheese 185
Fruit. *See also* specific fruit
  Apple Pineapple Salad 68
  Berries from the Trail with Custard Sauce 241
  Christmas Stewed Fruit 67
  Dessert Soup 242
  Piña Colada Fruit Salad 68
  Pistachio Ambrosia Salad 66

G

Garden Patch Soup 45
Garlic-Cheese Spread 19
Garlic Roasted Asparagus 92
General Store Café Wild Rice Apple Salad 52

Gingersnaps, Pepparkakor 222
Golden Beans Au Gratin 105
Gooey Chex Mix 236
Grandma's Baked Alaska 231
Granny's Applesauce Meatloaf 141
Gravy. *See* Sauces
Grilled Bacon-Wrapped Waterfowl 138
Grilled Fish 169
Guacamole, Fresh 13

H

Halibut, Zesty 171
Ham
    Ham and Dill Pickle Appetizer Bites 22
    Hunter's Stew 48
    Scalloped Potatoes 99
Hamburger Pie 151
Harvest Apple Pie 192
He-Man's Stew 50
Hibernation Fry Bread 82
Hockey Skins 26
Honey-Mustard Glazed Carrots 102
Honey Wheat Bread 74
Hot Corn Dip 10
Hot Island Russian Lullaby Tea 28
Hummus 18
Hungarian Goulash 151
Hunter's Stew 48

I

Ice Cream
    Grandma's Baked Alaska 231
    Nano Ice Cream 232
    Polar Pete's Baked Alaska 230
    Sweet and Spiced Coffee 33
    Yukon Yummies 234
Italian Stuffed Peppers 149
Italian Zucchini Pie 117

J

Jalapeños, Pickled 22
Janet Bennett's Bumstead's 70
Jumbo Shells 140

K

Kahlúa Bread 81
Kerin Fahland 160
Key's Café All American Apple Pie 193
Kringle 240

L

Leeks, Potatoes with 97
Lefse 89
Lefse, Bucky's 90
Lemon
    Lemon Poppy Seed Bread 81
    Lemon Shrimp 169
    Punch for a Crowd 32
    Wassail 34
    Zesty Halibut 171
Limpa 75
Lush Angel Dessert 241

M

Mango, Pork Medallions with 157
Maple
    Maple Apple Crisp 208
    Maple Baked Oatmeal 244
    Maple Glazed Sweet Potatoes with Bacon and
        Caramelized Onions 115
    Vermont Maple Pecan Cookies 218
Marinade 176
Marinated Chicken Wings 127
Max's Potatoes 96
Meatballs
    Delicious Barbecued Meatballs 142
    Swedish Meatballs with Gravy 142
    Sweet-N-Sour Meatballs 143

Meatloaf
    Granny's Applesauce Meatloaf 141
    Meatloaf 141
    Pheasant Meatloaf 138
Mexican Goulash 118
Miniature Blueberry Cheesecakes 187
Minnesota Blueberry Muffins 76
Minnes"O"ta Cucumber Salad 63
Minnesota Vacation Chicken Wild Rice Soup 38
Minotte's Steak Sinatra 154
Mocha Cooler 34
Monster Cookies 219
Mousse, Chocolate 227
Muffins
    Corn Muffins 79
    Minnesota Blueberry Muffins 76
    Orange Glazed Mini Muffins 77
    Pecan Pie Mini Muffins 78
Mushrooms
    Asparagus, Mushroom/Gorgonzola Risotto 93
    Beef Stroganoff 145
    Chicken Crêpes 132
    Chicken Tetrazzini 133
    Hunter's Stew 48
    Lemon Shrimp 169
    Minnesota Vacation Chicken Wild Rice Soup 38
    Minotte's Steak Sinatra 154
    Pete's Reindeer Stew 47
    Pheasant Meatloaf 138
    Polish Hotdish 150
    Sally's Wild Rice Soup 37
    Slow Cooker Chicken in Mushroom Gravy 131
    Spaghetti with Fresh Vegetables Sauce 121
    Spinach Salad 59
    Stuffed Mushrooms 94
    Stuffed Peppers 148
    Thyme Mushroom Gravy 175
    Venison Stroganoff 161
    Wild Rice Soup 36

N

Nano Ice Cream 232
No Crust Pumpkin Pie 197
Noodles. *See* Pasta
North Country Basting Sauce 176
Norwegian Apple Pie 192

O

Oats
    Apple Oatmeal Crisp 203
    Apple Pizza 229
    Bear Paw Resort's Rhubarb Crunch 201
    Delicious Barbecued Meatballs 142
    Maple Baked Oatmeal 244
    Monster Cookies 219
    Oatmeal Carmelitas 210
    Oatmeal Cookies 224
    O'Henry Bars 212
    Peanut Butter Fingers 213
    Rhubarb Crunch 200
    Vermont Maple Pecan Cookies 218
O'Henry Bars 212
Orange
    Brazilian Black Bean Soup 43
    Dakota Day Wild Rice Salad 54
    Hot Island Russian Lullaby Tea 28
    Orange Glazed Mini Muffins 77
    Pistachio Ambrosia Salad 66
    Punch for a Crowd 32
    Wassail 34
Oriental Chicken Wings 26
Oyster Stew, Appeldoorn's 46

P

Pancakes
    Banana Pancakes 87
    French Potato Pancakes 86
    Potato Pancakes 86
    Pumpkin Pancakes 87
    Swedish Bacon Pancake 88

Party Sandwiches 27
Pasta
    Axel's Spicy Penne 136
    Better-For-You Mac & Cheese 123
    Chicken Tetrazzini 133
    Chinese Noodle Casserole 153
    Cove Point's Lucca Pasta 137
    Jumbo Shells 140
    Lemon Shrimp 169
    Mexican Goulash 118
    Minnes"O"ta Cucumber Salad 63
    Polish Hotdish 150
    "Real" Mac & Cheese 122
    Spaghetti with Fresh Vegetables Sauce 121
    Tortellini Cranberry Salad 66
Paté, Smoked Trout 20
Pat's Crumble Burgers 147
Peanut Butter
    Buckeye Brownies 216
    Monster Cookies 219
    O'Henry Bars 212
    Peanut Butter Fingers 213
    Peanut Butter Squares 213
    Special K Bars 214
Peas
    Better-For-You Mac & Cheese 123
    He-Man's Stew 50
    Mexican Goulash 118
    Shrimp and Pea Rice Bowl 168
    Split Pea Soup 44
    Texas Salsa 12
Pecans
    Apple Pineapple Salad 68
    County Fair Chicken Bake 128
    Fresh Apple Cake 191
    Pecan Apple Pie 195
    Pecan Pie Mini Muffins 78
    Pheasant Meatloaf 138
    Salmon Party Log 21
    Vermont Maple Pecan Cookies 218

Pembroke Bakery's Favorite Chocolate Krinkles 221
Pepparkakor (Spice or Gingersnaps) 222
Pepperoni Pizza Pita Pockets 23
Pete's Reindeer Stew 47
Pheasant Meatloaf 138
Pickled Jalapeños 22
Pies
    Basic Pie Crust 194
    Butterfinger Cream Pie 198
    Buttermilk Pie 194
    Hamburger Pie 151
    Harvest Apple Pie 192
    Italian Zucchini Pie 117
    Key's Café All American Apple Pie 193
    No Crust Pumpkin Pie 197
    Norwegian Apple Pie 192
    Pecan Apple Pie 195
    Pumpkin Cream Cheese Pie 197
    Shoo-Fly Pie 196
Piña Colada Fruit Salad 68
Pineapple
    Apple Pineapple Salad 68
    Hot Island Russian Lullaby Tea 28
    Marinated Chicken Wings 127
    Piña Colada Fruit Salad 68
    Pistachio Ambrosia Salad 66
    Punch for a Crowd 32
    Tantalizing Tilapia 163
    Teriyaki Chicken Wings 127
    Wassail 34
    Zucchini Bread 80
Pistachio Ambrosia Salad 66
Pistachio Spread, Feta Cheese and 16
Pizza
    Apple Pizza 229
    Easter Pizza 124
    Pepperoni Pizza Pita Pockets 23
Pleasin' Popovers 72
Polar Pete's Baked Alaska 230
Polish Hotdish 150

Popcorn Salad, Carnival 69
Popovers 72
Poppy Seed Dressing 55
Pork. *See also* Ham, Sausage
    Beef and Pork Roast 156
    Bob Lauer's Father's Rib Recipe 159
    Cabbage Rolls 152
    Country-Style Pork Ribs 160
    Meatloaf 141
    Pork Chops and Apples 158
    Pork Medallions with Mango 157
    Swedish Meatballs with Gravy 142
Potatoes
    Baked Breakfast Hash Browns 95
    Beef and Pork Roast 156
    Bucky's Lefse 90
    Cabbage Soup 39
    Cheesy Potato Slices 99
    Crockpot Beef Stew 50
    Do-Ahead Garlic Mashed Potatoes 100
    French Potato Pancakes 86
    Garden Patch Soup 45
    Hamburger Pie 151
    He-Man's Stew 50
    Hockey Skins 26
    Hungarian Goulash 151
    Lefse 89
    Max's Potatoes 96
    Potato-Crusted Walleye with Cucumber Sour
        Cream Dressing 164
    Potatoes with Leeks 97
    Potato Pancakes 86
    Roller Coaster Potato Salad 65
    Rosemary Roman Potatoes 98
    Scalloped Potatoes 99
    Tater Tot Hot Dish 94
    Winter's Day Seasoned Potatoes 101
Poultry. *See* Chicken and Turkey
Pound Cake for Choco-holics 184

Pudding
    Chocolate Bread Pudding 225
    Chocolate Mousse 227
    Cold Yogurt Pumpkin Pudding 226
    Pumpkin Fluff 226
Pumpkin
    Cold Yogurt Pumpkin Pudding 226
    No Crust Pumpkin Pie 197
    Pumpkin Cream Cheese Pie 197
    Pumpkin Dessert 209
    Pumpkin Fluff 226
    Pumpkin Pancakes 87
Punch
    Champagne Punch 32
    Punch for a Crowd 32
    Wassail 34

Q

Quinoa with Fish 170

R

Ramen Noodle Salad 61
Raspberry
    Berries from the Trail with Custard Sauce 241
    Piña Colada Fruit Salad 68
    Raspberry Infusion Cocktail 31
"Real" Mac & Cheese 122
Reindeer Stew, Pete's 47
Rhubarb
    Bear Paw Resort's Rhubarb Crunch 201
    Rhubarb Cake 188
    Rhubarb Crunch 200
    Rhubarb Slush 29
Ribs
    Bob Lauer's Father's Rib Recipe 159
    Country-Style Pork Ribs 160
Rice. *See also* Wild Rice
    Asparagus, Mushroom/Gorgonzola Risotto 93
    Cabbage Rolls 152
    Chicken Hotdish 130
    Chicken Stir-Fry 126

Chinese Noodle Casserole 153
Deluxe Hotdish 134
Italian Stuffed Peppers 149
Potato-Crusted Walleye with Cucumber Sour
    Cream Dressing 164
Shrimp and Pea Rice Bowl 168
Stuffed Peppers 148
Tantalizing Tilapia 163
Texas Hash 144
Roasted Pumpkin Seeds 24
Roller Coaster Potato Salad 65
Rommegrot 243
Rosemary and Garlic Roasted Chicken 129
Rosemary Roman Potatoes 98

S

Salads. *See also* Coleslaw
    Apple Pineapple Salad 68
    Apple-Romaine Salad 58
    Apple-Walnut Salad 58
    Baby Corn Salad 65
    Carnival Popcorn Salad 69
    Christmas Stewed Fruit 67
    Dakota Day Wild Rice Salad 54
    Fresh Green Salad with Almonds & Craisins 57
    General Store Café Wild Rice Apple Salad 52
    Minnes"O"ta Cucumber Salad 63
    Piña Colada Fruit Salad 68
    Pistachio Ambrosia Salad 66
    Ramen Noodle Salad 61
    Roller Coaster Potato Salad 65
    Spinach Salad 59
    Spring Salad 55
    Taco Salad 60
    Tortellini Cranberry Salad 66
    Wild Rice and Edamame Salad 53
Sally's Wild Rice Soup 37
Salmon
    Bourbon Planked Salmon 167
    Fish Pond Salmon Spread 21
    Grilled Fish 169

Salmon Party Log 21
Salmon Sandwich Bake 166
Sandwiches
    French Dip 155
    Janet Bennett's Bumstead's 70
    Party Sandwiches 27
    Pat's Crumble Burgers 147
    Salmon Sandwich Bake 166
    Sloppy Joes 146
    Tavern Burgers 146
Sauces
    Béarnaise Sauce 172
    Best-Ever Brown Gravy 174
    Chinese Brown Gravy 175
    Kahlúa Sauce 225
    Mornay Sauce 132
    North Country Basting Sauce 176
    Thyme Mushroom Gravy 175
Sausage
    Cabbage Soup 39
    Chinese Noodle Casserole 153
    Hunter's Stew 48
    Taco Party Dip 13
Scalloped Potatoes 99
Seafood. *See* specific seafood
Shoo-Fly Pie 196
Shrimp
    Lemon Shrimp 169
    Shrimp and Pea Rice Bowl 168
    Tantalizing Tilapia 163
Sinclair Lewis' Sinful Christmas Cookies 220
Sloppy Joes 146
Slow Cooker Chicken in Mushroom Gravy 131
Slow Cooker Stuffing 120
Smoked Trout Paté 20
S'mores Brownie Cake 183
Snickerdoodle Bars 211
Snicker's Cake 180
Soul Cakes 83

Soups
    Brazilian Black Bean Soup 43
    Broccoli Cheese Soup 41
    Cabbage Soup 39
    Chilly Day Wild Rice Soup 36
    Crockpot Beer Cheese Soup 42
    Dessert Soup 242
    Garden Patch Soup 45
    Minnesota Vacation Chicken Wild Rice Soup 38
    Sally's Wild Rice Soup 37
    Split Pea Soup 44
    Tomato Basil Soup 40
    Wild Rice Soup 36
Spaghetti with Fresh Vegetables Sauce 121
Special K Bars 214
Spicy Minnesota Spread 17
Spinach
    Blackened Swordfish 172
    Spinach Salad 59
    Tantalizing Tilapia 163
Split Pea Soup 44
Spreads. *See* Appetizers
Spring Salad 55
Squaw Corn 106
Stew
    Appeldoorn's Oyster Stew 46
    Crockpot Beef Stew 50
    He-Man's Stew 50
    Hunter's Stew 48
    Pete's Reindeer Stew 47
Strawberry
    Easy Strawberry Cake 189
    Piña Colada Fruit Salad 68
    Strawberry Short Cake 190
Streusel Coffee Cake 179
Stuffed Artichokes 113
Stuffed Mushrooms 94
Stuffed Peppers 148
Swedish Almond Toast 84
Swedish Bacon Pancake 88
Swedish Meatballs with Gravy 142

Swedish Rye Bread 75
Sweet and Spiced Coffee 33
Sweet-N-Sour Meatballs 143
Sweet Potato Apple Casserole 114
Sweet Potatoes with Bacon and Caramelized
    Onions, Maple Glazed 115
Swordfish, Blackened 172

T

Taco Party Dip 13
Taco Salad 60
Tantalizing Tilapia 163
Tasty Tilapia 162
Tater Tot Hot Dish 94
Tavern Burgers 146
Teriyaki Chicken Wings 127
Texas Hash 144
Texas Salsa 12
Thyme Mushroom Gravy 175
Tilapia
    Grilled Fish 169
    Quinoa with Fish 170
    Tantalizing Tilapia 163
    Tasty Tilapia 162
Toasted Almond Party Spread 16
Tomato and Corn Scallop 107
Tomato Basil Soup 40
Tortellini Cranberry Salad 66
Tortes, Chocolate Port Cheesecake 235
Trout Paté, Smoked 20
Truffles, Blue Cashew 25
Tuna, Janet Bennett's Bumstead's 70
Turkey, Pheasant Meatloaf 138

V

Vegetables. *See also* specific vegetable
    Crockpot Beef Stew 50
    Garden Patch Soup 45
    He-Man's Stew 50
    Mexican Goulash 118
    Spaghetti with Fresh Vegetables Sauce 121

Venison Stroganoff 161
Vension, Kerin Fahland 160
Vermont Maple Pecan Cookies 218

W

Walleye Cakes 165
Walleye with Cucumber Sour Cream Dressing,
    Potato-Crusted 164
Walnut
    Apple-Walnut Salad 58
    Baklava 223
    Cold Yogurt Pumpkin Pudding 226
    Fresh Apple Cake 191
    Pumpkin Dessert 209
    Walnut Chicken Spread 19
    Zucchini Bread 80
Wassail 34
Watermelon, Coolers 30
Wedding Cake 180
White Chicken Chili 51
White Christmas Mix 237

Wild Rice
    Chilly Day Wild Rice Soup 36
    County Fair Chicken Bake 128
    Dakota Day Wild Rice Salad 54
    Deluxe Hotdish 134
    General Store Café Wild Rice Apple Salad 52
    Sally's Wild Rice Soup 37
    Wild Rice and Edamame Salad 53
    Wild Rice Krispy Bars 215
    Wild Rice Soup 36
    Wild Rice & Toasted Almond Pilaf 119
Winter's Day Seasoned Potatoes 101

Y

Yukon Yummies 234

Z

Zesty Halibut 171
Zig's Hot Artichoke Dip 15
Zucchini
    Italian Zucchini Pie 117
    Spaghetti with Fresh Vegetables Sauce 121
    Zucchini Bread 80

Pleasant Valley Orchard

Recipe Notes

Travel Plans

About the Author:

In 1999, Christy Campbell began her journey in the world of cookbooks when she took a position at a publishing company specializing in regional cookbooks. At the time, it was an all-new experience, so she immersed herself in cookbooks, both at home and at the office. With the help of the associate publisher and her personal mentor, Sheila Simmons (author, STATE HOMETOWN COOKBOOK SERIES), Christy learned the in's and out's of the small press world, devoting herself to cookbooks for the next 6 years. After the birth of her youngest son, Campbell took a sabbatical from the publishing world to focus on her young family.

In 2009, Campbell reconnected with Sheila Simmons and began work with Great American Publishers, reenergizing a 10 year love of cookbooks. She is now an integral part of Great American Publishers and has begun a new cookbook series of her own. The EAT & EXPLORE STATE COOKBOOK SERIES chronicles the favorite recipes of local cooks across the United States while highlighting the most popular events and destinations in each state.

When she is not writing cookbooks, selling cookbooks or cooking recipes for cookbooks, Christy Campbell enjoys volunteering at her children's school, running and reading. She lives in Brandon, Mississippi, with her husband Michael and their two sons.

State Hometown Cookbook Series
A Hometown Taste of America, One State at a Time
EACH: $18.95 • 240 to 272 pages • 8x9 • paperbound

The STATE HOMETOWN COOKBOOK SERIES captures each state's hometown charm by combining great-tasting local recipes from real hometown cooks with interesting stories and photos from festivals all over the state. As a souvenir, gift, or collector's item, this unique series is sure to take you back to your hometown... or take you on a journey to explore other hometowns across the country.

Georgia Hometown Cookbook • 978-1-934817-01-8

Louisiana Hometown Cookbook • 978-1-934817-07-0

Mississippi Hometown Cookbook • 978-1-934817-08-7

South Carolina Hometown Cookbook • 978-1-934817-10-0

Tennessee Hometown Cookbook • 978-0-9779053-2-4

Texas Hometown Cookbook • 978-1-934817-04-9

- Easy to follow recipes produce great-tasting dishes every time.
- Recipes use ingredients you probably already have in your pantry.
- Fun-to-read sidebars feature food-related festivals across the state.
- The perfect gift for anyone who loves to cook.
- Makes a great souvenir.

Family Favorite Recipes

It's so easy to cook great food your family will love with 350 simply delicious recipes for easy-to-afford, easy-to-prepare dinners. From **Great Grandmother's Coconut Pie**, to **Granny's Vanilla Wafer Cake** to **Mama's Red Beans & Rice**, this outstanding cookbook is the result of decades of cooking and collecting recipes. It's so easy to encourage your family to eat more meals at home...to enjoy time spent in the kitchen... to save money making delicious affordable meals...to cook the foods your family loves without the fuss...with *Family Favorite Recipes*.

$18.95 • 248 pages • 7x10 • paperbound • 978-1-934817-14-8

www.GreatAmericanPublishers.com • www.facebook.com/GreatAmericanPublishers

Eat & Explore Cookbook Series

EAT AND EXPLORE STATE COOKBOOK SERIES is a favorite of local cooks, arm-chair travelers and cookbook collectors across the United States. Call us toll-free 1.888.854.5954 to order additional copies or to join our Cookbook Club.

EACH: **$18.95 • 240 to 272 pages • 7x9 • paperbound**

Now Available...   **Coming Soon...**

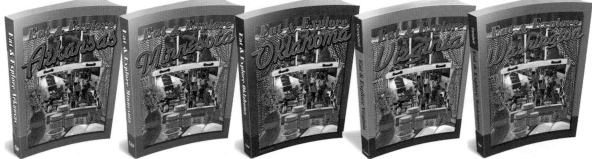

Arkansas	**Minnesota**	**Oklahoma**	**Virginia**	**Washington**
978-1-934817-09-4	978-1-934817-15-5	978-1-934817-11-7	978-1-934817-12-4	978-1-934817-16-2

Don't miss out on our upcoming titles—join our Cookbook Club and you'll be notified of each new edition.

www.GreatAmericanPublishers.com • www.facebook.com/GreatAmericanPublishers

---

Order Form Mail to: Great American Publishers • P. O. Box 1305 • Kosciusko, MS 39090
Or call us toll-free 1.888.854.5954 to order by check or credit card

❑ Check Enclosed
Charge to: ❑ Visa ❑ MC ❑ AmEx ❑ Disc

Card # _____

Exp Date _____ Signature _____

Name _____

Address _____

City _____ State _____

Zip _____

Phone _____

Email _____

Qty.	Title	Total
	Subtotal	
	Postage ($3 first book; $0.50 each additional)	
	Total	